Deborah Osborne, MA
Susan Wernicke, MS

Introduction
to Crime Analysis
Basic Resources
for Criminal Justice Practice

Pre-publication
REVIEWS,
COMMENTARIES,
EVALUATIONS . . .

"**E**very crime analyst needs resources. This book is packed with listings that will benefit both new and seasoned analysts alike. Deborah Osborne and Susan Wernicke are knowledgeable crime analysts who are intimately familiar with the material covered in this book. I appreciate their dedication to our profession."

Steven Gottlieb, MPA
Executive Director,
Alpha Group Center for Crime
and Intelligence Analysis Training,
Montclair, California;
Primary author, *Crime Analysis:*
From First Report to Final Arrest

"**F**or those of us involved in the day-to-day education and training of crime and intelligence analysts there is a sad lack of serious literature that helps us in our task. *Introduction to Crime Analysis: Basic Resources for Criminal Justice Practice* helps fill that void. Following a logical path, the authors provide definitions, tools, practical examples, resources, and the broad overview needed to function as a crime analyst, particularly in a small- to medium-sized police department.

This very readable book will mesh nicely with formalized crime analyst training and should be on the purchase list of apprentices and journeymen. It also provides an excellent perspective for supervisors and managers. I highly recommend it."

Robert J. Heibel, MLS
Director, Research/Intelligence
Analyst Program,
Mercyhurst College,
Erie, Pennsylvania

The Haworth Press®
New York • London • Oxford

Introduction
to Crime Analysis
Basic Resources
for Criminal Justice Practice

THE HAWORTH PRESS
Titles of Related Interest

Introduction to Crime Analysis
Basic Resources for Criminal Justice Practice

Deborah Osborne, MA
Susan Wernicke, MS

The Haworth Press®
New York • London • Oxford

The Haworth Press, Inc. 10 Alice Street, Binghamton, NY 13904-1580.

PUBLISHER'S NOTE
Due to the ever-changing nature of the Internet, Web site names and addresses, though verified to the best of the publisher's ability, should not be accepted as accurate without independent verification.

Cover design by Brooke R. Stiles.

Library of Congress Cataloging-in-Publication Data

Osborne, Deborah.
    Introduction to crime analysis : basic resources for criminal justice practice / Deborah Osborne, Susan Wernicke.
        p. cm.
Includes bibliographical references and index.
    ISBN 0-7890-1867-5 (harcover : alk. paper)—ISBN 0-7890-1868-3 (softcover : alk. paper)
1. Crime analysis. I. Wernicke, Susan. II. Title.
    HV7936.C88 O83 2003
    363.25—dc21
                                                                                2002151526

This book is dedicated to our families,
with great love and thanks,
and to the protectors of all families:
our local law enforcers.

ABOUT THE AUTHORS

Deborah Osborne is a crime analyst for the Buffalo Police Department and co-founder/vice president of the Western New York Regional Association of Crime and Intelligence Analysts. She serves on the by-laws committee and the certification committee of the International Association of Crime Analysts (IACA). She is a state certified police instructor and has served as an independent consultant to the Police Service of Northern Ireland (formerly RUC). Ms. Osborne holds a BA in Psychology and an MA in Social Policy.

Susan Wernicke has set up a crime analysis unit for the Shawnee Police Department after working ten years for the Overland Park, Kansas, Police Department. During her tenure at the Overland Park Police Department, she held the positions of communications officer, police report clerk, and crime analyst. She has contributed to various publications on crime mapping, including *Crime Mapping Successes in the Field,* Volumes I and II, and *Crime Mapping: Principal and Practice.* She has also authored various articles on crime analysis, including an article for *The Police Chief* magazine titled "Integrating Crime Analysis into Local Law Enforcement." Ms. Wernicke is the former Training Coordinator for the Mid-America Regional Crime Analysis Network (MARCAN) and is a crime analysis instructor for the International Association of Chiefs of Police (IACP). She is also the Secretary on the Executive Board for the International Association of Crime Analysts (IACA). She serves as the Committee Chair for the Publications Committee and for the Training Series Oversight and Implementation Committee. In December 2001, Ms. Wernicke was the keynote speaker at the Florida Crime and Intelligence Analysts Association (FCIAA) as well as the Conference Chairperson for the 2001 IACA Training Conference. She holds a BS in Human Services/Criminal Justice and an MS in Management.

CONTENTS

Preface

Knowledge is power.
Sir Francis Bacon

Introduction to Crime Analysis is a practical guide and resource for anyone working in law enforcement who has the responsibility of analyzing crime. The newly hired crime analyst, the police officer responsible for addressing crime problems and patterns in community problem-solving efforts, the investigator probing serial crimes, or the police manager responsible for identifying crime problems in his or her command—this book is written to assist you in your efforts. Although our target audience is the individual new to crime analysis, this book offers a number of resources that will be helpful to any working analyst, no matter how experienced and knowledgeable.

The emphasis of this book is practical rather than theoretical. *Introduction to Crime Analysis* refers to the role of the crime analyst or analyst, but since many smaller police agencies cannot justify hiring a full-time analyst, the authors suggest that any police officer reading this book substitute "officer" in place of "analyst." Considering that, according to the Bureau of Justice Statistics, there are over 13,000 local law enforcement agencies in the United States and, as of June 1999, only forty-six of these departments employed 1,000 or more officers, in many agencies the responsibility for crime analysis falls on officers' shoulders.

Most of this book is written in the second person to help you, the individual new to crime analysis. The first chapter will introduce you to crime analysis, the challenges of defining crime analysis, the reasons to analyze crime, and the basic types of crime analysis in local law enforcement.

The second chapter discusses the tools of crime analysis and will provide you with some ideas for improving your skills and knowledge base. Computer skills are a must for crime analysts and, since many of the resources in this book are linked to Internet sites, having computer skills will help you access a wealth of free information in cyberspace.

The third chapter will teach you about the stages of crime analysis, using tactical crime analysis examples. Implementing the stages of crime analysis will help you begin to analyze crime in your agency, step by step. This chapter will tell you how to analyze crime even if your agency does not have advanced technology.

The fourth chapter will introduce you to some issues in crime mapping and provide you with resources to get started. Introduction to common crime analysis products, preparation instructions, and guidance are provided in the fifth chapter. The sixth chapter of this book gives tips for beginning crime analysts, as well as information on relevant associations and resources.

The seventh chapter is an overview on issues involved in creating a new crime analysis unit, including recommendations from the field. If you are the only analyst in a law enforcement agency, this chapter is still relevant. For example, you will find tips on using interns and volunteers to help you create a working "unit." Crime Analysis Success Stories are also provided from working analysts to get perspectives from the field.

Chapter 8 lists training and education resources, both for those working in law enforcement and those who are not. Chapter 9 concludes with other agencies, publications, and Internet sites that may be valuable to you in expanding your knowledge base.

Crime analysis is important work! Criminals know no jurisdictional boundaries, have no bureaucracy to struggle with, and no funding woes. Criminals have access to the newest technology and are eager to take advantage of every flaw in the law enforcement system. In the United States, we are especially conscious of threats to national security in the aftermath of the September 11, 2001, terrorist attacks. Analyzing crime at the local, state, and federal levels and sharing the knowledge that is distilled from this information, thus increasing public safety, are of paramount concern to all of us. Crime analysis is a set of valuable methods using the tool of the human intellect in policing to help address crime and national security problems with innovative solutions.

Military strategists have used analysis for centuries; it makes sense to know as much about the enemy and about the conditions and causes of a situation if we hope to institute any kind of significant change for the better. Career criminals are enemies of a community's well-being. Now that advances in information technology give us the means and methods to more fully examine and find meaningful knowledge in the vast amounts of existing information on crimes and criminals— information that was too cumbersome and difficult to search in the past—we are obligated to use our technological strength to protect innocent people. Systematic crime analysis as a law enforcement and public safety asset has become not only possible but also truly necessary as a weapon in the war against crime.

Acknowledgments

Many persons contributed information and ideas to this book. We would like to thank the following individuals and their agencies for responding to a questionnaire we created in order to discover what others are doing in the field of crime analysis so we could pass this information along to our readers:

- Megan Ambrosio, Newark Police Department, New Jersey
- Michelle Arneson, Green Bay Police Department, Wisconsin
- Paul Bentley, Scottsdale Police Department, Arizona
- Christopher Bruce, Cambridge Police Department, Massachusetts (now with Danvers PD)
- Chief of Police Tom Casady, Lincoln Police Department, Nebraska
- John Couchell and Monica Nguyen, Charlotte-Mecklenburg Police Department, North Carolina
- Brian Cummings, Richmond Police Department, Virginia
- Lieutenant Thomas Evans, Pinellas County Sheriff's Department, Florida
- John Gottschalk, Pierce County Sheriff's Department, Washington
- Anne Gunther, Hampton Police Division, Virginia
- Dan Helms, Las Vegas Metropolitan Police Department, Nevada
- Detective Bryan Hill, Phoenix Police Department, Arizona
- Al Johnson, Austin Police Department, Texas
- John Laws, Portland Police Bureau, Oregon
- Ken Maly, Aaron Otto, and Detective Steve Libby, Akron Police Department, Ohio
- Carol McCoy, Lenexa Police Department, Kansas
- Charlotte Quintana, Mesa Police Department, Arizona
- Mel Rhamey, Boulder Police Department, Colorado
- Eugenia Johnson Smith, Lexington Police, Kentucky

- Riley Spoon and Yvetta Thomas, Winston-Salem Police Department, North Carolina
- Sergeant Mark Stallo, Dallas Police Department, Texas
- Richard Strait, Savannah Police Department, Georgia
- Gerald Tallman and Jamie May, Overland Park Police Department, Kansas
- Senior Officer Dale Wood, Oceanside Police Department, California
- Lieutenant Michael Wood, Rochester Police Department, New York

To the individuals who contributed articles to this book, much thanks and appreciation! These individuals include:

- Sergeant Dan Barber of the Boulder County Sheriff's Department for his success story
- Cheri Cohn, formerly of the Lakewood Police Department for her "A Day in the Life of a Crime Analyst"
- Christopher Bruce of the Danvers Police Department for allowing us to print his "Ten Commandments for Crime Analysis"
- Mel Rhamey of the Boulder Police Department for her story on achieving credibility as a crime analyst
- Doug Rains of Aurora, Colorado, for his success story
- Chris Gephardt and Don Fagging for help in equipment requirements and statistics

Many thanks to all the generous individuals working in this interesting and challenging field—all those willing to share ideas and expertise at conferences, on the Internet, and by telephone. Special thanks to crime analysts Andrea Might of Peel Regional Police and Michelle Arneson of Green Bay Police for their encouragement during the early stages of the book-writing process.

Thank you to Steve Gottlieb for saying this book was a good idea before a word was written. Thanks to Mark Evans, Gerald Schoenle, Thomas Nowak, Kim Rossmo, Mark Stallo, Robert Heibel, Patricia Saber, and many others for encouragement and guidance.

Our most sincere thanks to our loved ones, who endured the book-writing process with understanding and patience. Thank you!

Chapter 1

What Is Crime Analysis?

THE CHALLENGE OF DEFINING CRIME ANALYSIS

Advances in technology, which allow analyses of large quantities of data, are the foundation for the relatively new field known as *crime analysis*. Crime analysis is an emerging field in law enforcement without standard definitions. This makes it difficult to determine the crime analysis focus for agencies that are new to the field. In some police departments, what is called "crime analysis" consists of mapping crimes for command staff and producing crime statistics. In other agencies, crime analysis might mean focusing on analyzing various police reports and suspect information to help investigators in major crime units identify serial robbers and sex offenders. Some analysts do all this and other types of analysis. The role of the crime analyst varies from agency to agency.

Crime analysis is the act of analyzing crime. More specifically, crime analysis is the breaking up of acts committed in violation of laws into their parts to find out their nature and reporting statements of these findings. The objective of most crime analysis is to find meaningful information in vast amounts of data and disseminate this information to officers and investigators in the field to assist in their efforts to apprehend criminals and suppress criminal activity. Assessing crime through analysis also helps in crime prevention efforts. Preventing crime costs less than trying to apprehend criminals after crimes occur.

A leading textbook for crime analysis, *Crime Analysis: From First Report to Final Arrest,* was first printed in 1994. In this text, crime analysis is defined as follows:

Crime analysis is defined as a set of systematic, analytical processes directed at providing timely and pertinent information relative to crime patterns and trend correlations to assist operational and administrative personnel in planning the deployment of resources for the prevention and suppression of criminal activities, aiding the investigative process, and increasing apprehensions and the clearance of cases. Within this context, crime analysis supports a number of department functions including patrol deployment, special operations and tactical units, investigations, planning and research, crime prevention, and administrative services (budgeting and program planning). (Gottlieb, Arenberg, and Singh 1994, 13)

You will find that there are many misconceptions about crime analysis. Those who do not work in law enforcement may think the crime analyst is either a criminalist, an individual who goes to crime scenes to collect and analyze evidence; a criminologist, an individual who studies criminal behavior; or a psychological profiler, an individual who does in-depth psychological analysis of serial criminals.

Within law enforcement there are other widespread misconceptions about the role of the crime analyst. A crime analyst may primarily be seen as a statistician or "numbers cruncher." This is a common misconception arising from the fact that statistics are used in analyzing crime, but as only one tool in trying to uncover crime problems and detect patterns and relationships among variables. Crime analysis is much more than statistics. Focusing on statistics alone is shortsighted and limits the potential of crime analysis in a police agency.

The rich information resources of a police department are basically untapped if no one is available to analyze crime as it occurs, on a daily basis, to help officers catch the criminal who is committing crimes right now. Providing crime statistics for police administrators is important, but it should not be the only focus of a crime analysis unit. Crime analysis can support decision making, problem solving, and strategy planning at every level of policing.

THE PRESENT STATE OF CRIME ANALYSIS
IN LAW ENFORCEMENT

Today, agencies range from those having no formal crime analysis at all to others having very sophisticated units with analysts specializing in certain types of crimes or assigned to geographical chapters of a city, county, or state. Some agencies have analysts using manual ledgers with handwritten notes on suspect data, modus operandi (MO) factors, and other crucial data while others have separate databases for everything from violent crimes such as homicides and sex offenses to construction-site theft. Many agencies do not have automated crime mapping and rely on using the old-fashioned pin maps while awaiting grant funds, a new budget year, or some other way of funding the purchase of the appropriate software. Other technologically sophisticated agencies take for granted automated pin mapping, thematic mapping, and spatial analysis and are looking at new innovative technologies such as three-dimensional mapping, mapping on the Web, and animated maps as goals for the upcoming fiscal year.

Although this book focuses on assisting North American crime analysts and those officers charged with analyzing crimes at the local law enforcement level, the authors are aware of the emerging interest in crime analysis at other levels of government and in other countries throughout the world. The United Kingdom's National Criminal Intelligence Service has instituted a comprehensive policy change in policing at every level that emphasizes analysis at the center of law enforcement endeavors (National Criminal Intelligence Service 2000). The FBI is in the process of developing core competencies and standards for their intelligence analysts (Burton 2000). In June 2000, a group of intelligence trainers and intelligence leaders from around the world met at Mercyhurst College in Erie, Pennsylvania, to discuss developing transnational standards for intelligence analysts. The awareness of the benefits of analyzing information in policing and the need for trained crime and intelligence analysts are being realized by many agencies simultaneously. This is a significant time of growth and recognition for the profession of law enforcement analysis.

The International Association of Crime Analysts (IACA) is currently working on several projects in an effort to move the profession forward. These include, but are not limited to, international certification of analysts, the development of IACA chapters (most likely utilizing current state and regional associations as charter chapters), the development of the Web site to include FAQs, job opportunities, IACA project status, membership development, and other crime analysis and mapping-related opportunities, information, and projects. Membership within the professional organization has skyrocketed over the past several years. The explosive growth in the formation of crime analysis units has sharply increased the need and demand for analysts. Training classes for crime analysis are easily filled as analysts and officers assigned to analysis seek any and every opportunity available to gain the needed skills to become successful crime analysts.

The undisputed trend toward civilianizing crime analysis units is clear. As crime analysis as a field first emerged, many agencies utilized police officers and/or detectives to fill crime analysis slots. Although many of the agencies believed that sworn officers would be the logical choice for crime analysts (noting their background and knowledge of criminal MOs and enterprises), many of these initial analysts lacked research skills and the computer skills necessary to manipulate and manage large databases of information and/or provide statistics and/or forecasting with accuracy and certainty. The move toward civilianizing the units, hiring individuals with research skills, computer skills, and police knowledge is heavily documented. Many larger departments today use a combination of civilian and sworn analysts, combining the strengths of both to create the ideal unit.

Crime analysts today are hungry for books, "white papers," articles, and training that provide guidance and direction in their crime analysis careers. The identification of this need for materials was what drove the authors to write this book.

WHY ANALYZE CRIME?

To help justify your existence as a crime analyst in your law enforcement agency to those who do not have an understanding of what the crime analyst does or what crime analysis can provide, it is important to be able to articulate some of the reasons it makes sense to analyze crime. Some good reasons are listed here. You will find other reasons as you progress in your work.

- Analyze crime to take advantage of the abundance of information existing in law enforcement agencies, the criminal justice system, and the public domain.

- Analyze crime to maximize the use of limited law enforcement resources.
- Analyze crime to inform law enforcers about general and specific crime trends, patterns, and series in an ongoing, timely manner.
- Analyze crime to have an objective means to access crime problems locally, regionally, statewide, nationally, and globally within and between law enforcement agencies.
- Analyze crime to be proactive in detecting and preventing crime.
- Analyze crime to meet the law enforcement needs of a changing society.

TYPES OF CRIME ANALYSIS

Tactical Crime Analysis

Tactical crime analysis involves analyzing data to develop information on the where, when, and how of crimes in order to assist officers and investigators in identifying and understanding specific and immediate crime problems. Tactical crime analysis units focus on and will work closely with patrol officers and investigators. The goal of tactical analysis is to promote a rapid response to a crime problem happening *right now.* One of your roles as a tactical crime analyst is to detect current patterns of criminal activity to predict possible future crime events.

Crime patterns are generally defined in geographic terms—a pattern of a specific crime type as clustered in a geographic area. However, a pattern of crime may transcend geography. A pattern implies similarities that are repeated, such as in a design. Therefore, for a crime type to exist in a pattern, it must have at least one variable that seems to repeat, whether it is location, time, target, or MO.

A crime series is a crime pattern wherein there is reason to believe the same person(s) committed the crimes. Identifying an existing crime series as early as possible is a primary mission of tactical crime analysis. By examining the MO pattern, the analyst can come to some conclusions regarding the dates, times, and locations of future criminal events committed in series. Tactical crime analysts develop general suspect and victim profiles based on data from various sources.

A good example of effective tactical crime analysis would be identification of a series as follows: liquor store robberies in a given geographic area wherein the suspect and MO information developed is similar. Similarities noted in these crimes include a white male suspect, in his twenties, 6'0", 180 pounds, with brown hair, wearing a ski mask and displaying a sawed-off shotgun, yelling for everyone to get down onto the ground, jumping the register, and taking the larger bills only. Several consecutive incidents matching this suspect description and MO information would constitute a crime series. An analyst discovering this series of crimes through analyzing data would be conducting tactical analysis.

Tactical crime analysis occurs in the present and the tactical crime analyst must be flexible in producing relevant crime analysis products. Modifications to reports must be made as new data that relate to a pattern or series become available. When an analyst prepares a tactical report, he or she should summarize the analysis conducted *and* include a suspect profile, victim profiles, MO factors, area or premise type, day and time preferred by the suspect, and other factors that may aid in identifying the perpetrator as he or she enters the area under surveillance. The desired result of tactical analysis is suspect apprehension through aggressive suspect and victim targeting and surveillance. Suggestions for tactical responses, such as increasing patrol in a certain area at a specific time period, may be part of a crime analysis report or bulletin.

Tactical crime analysis responses may also include altering the environment to prevent crimes. The concept of crime prevention through environmental design (CPTED) stresses changing the environment to prevent crime after careful analysis of environmental factors contributing to crime problems. A few examples of environmental factors contributing to burglaries might include poor lighting and overgrown shrubbery, accessibility for criminals to major thoroughfares as escape routes, and ineffective door locks. Some analysts, concerned about specific chronic or emerging crime problems, visit the physical area where the crimes have occurred to assess possible environmental contributing factors.

Recommendations to alter target victim behavior may also help prevent crime. If tactical crime analysis produces information that elderly females are being targeted for purse snatching in grocery store parking lots, the media can warn potential victims of this trend and possibly prevent future crimes.

Strategic Crime Analysis

Strategic crime analysis is concerned with long-range problems and planning for long-term projects. Strategic analysts examine long-term increases or decreases in crime, known as "crime trends." A crime trend is the direction of movement of crime and reflects either no change or increases/decreases in crime frequencies within a specific jurisdiction or area. For example, strategic analysts might study increased car thefts during the winter months when citizens warm up their cars, leaving them unlocked and unattended in various locations. Another example would be strategizing a plan of attack for decreasing "open-garage-door burglaries," which often take place during the summer when citizens leave their garage doors standing open for long periods of time, inviting burglars to walk into the structure and help themselves to expensive items.

Strategic crime analysts may provide information to crime prevention officers, community-oriented policing officers, planning and research, and community outreach programs. Together, the groups can work to identify overall increases in specific areas of crime, develop an action plan to address each issue, and work together to decrease the overall crime in particular areas, developments, complexes, business districts, or in the jurisdiction in general.

Crime analysts may be utilized in problem-oriented policing strategies and have much to offer in the "analysis" stage of this process. Analysts can be important resources in identification of problems at the start of the problem-oriented policing process.

Although strategic analysis is probably the least recognized type of analysis in public, government, or police sectors, it has been an integral part of the private sector for dozens of years. In the business world, strategic analysts note overall "trends" (good and bad), develop action plans to address these issues, and help by monitoring implementation of the plans. With the support and assistance of other divisions within the company as well as other companies, the community, and sometimes the government, private-sector companies use strategists to work toward ever-increasing success, particularly financial success.

Although public-sector agencies, specifically police departments, generally are not working to increase their financial success, analysts are working toward a measurable goal—the overall reduction of crime. Strategic crime analysts use "exception" reports to provide information to a variety of sources, from command staff and midlevel supervisors to line personnel and the community. These reports provide information on the "exception," the ongoing increase or decrease in particular crime categories, victim categories, target locations, or other crime elements of interest. Any deviation from the norm will be the focus of "exception" reports.

As government agencies adopt success strategies of businesses with the goal of saving money and maximizing resources, the importance of strategic crime analysis will become more recognized. The emphasis on becoming cost-effective and proactive in policing will require strategic analysis of crime and disorder problems as we move into the next millennium.

Administrative Crime Analysis

Administrative crime analysis focuses on providing summary data, statistics, and general trend information to police managers. This type of analysis involves providing descriptive information about crime to department administrators, command staff, and officers, as well as to other city government personnel and the public. Such reports provide support to administrators as they determine and allocate resources or help citizens to have a better understanding of the community crime and disorder problems. Number data provide measurable terms for crime and disorder problems and administrative analysis utilizes basic descriptive statistics to measure crime and calls for service in local law enforcement.

In some police agencies, crime analysts are responsible for administrative crime analysis involving monitoring and compiling statistics for the FBI Uniform Crime Report (UCR). In other agencies, UCR reporting is delegated to other staff members. Compiling such statistics generally involves little actual analysis.

Administrative crime analysis provides a range of services to a range of customers. Administrative crime analysis information can be significantly automated using technological resources. The automation of traditional administrative crime analysis tasks allows crime analysts to focus more on using their time and skills for tactical and strategic crime analysis.

Provision of crime comparisons showing a city's crime totals this year versus last year, this month versus last month, or this month, this year versus this month, last year is an example of administrative crime analysis. Administrative analysts also often use crime ratios to compare their city's crimes per 1,000 (or 10,000 or 100,000) to other cities of similar size and makeup. This is often referred to as *benchmarking*. Examples of administrative crime analysis products are included in Chapter 5 of this book.

Although tactical, strategic, and administrative crime analysis are often listed as the "three types of crime analysis," the types of analysis listed next are included in the current field of crime analysis.

Investigative Crime Analysis

Investigative crime analysis involves profiling suspects and victims for investigators based on analysis of available information. It is sometimes called "criminal investigative analysis." Generally, as conducted by crime analysts at the local law enforcement level, this is not the same type of intensive profiling done by the FBI for serial killers and rapists, but rather a more general hypothesizing about what type of person is committing a particular crime series.

In another method of investigative crime analysis, a crime analyst studies the aspects of profiling serial criminals such as serial burglars and serial robbers, interviews the investigators in various agencies for information on what types of persons commit certain crimes within specific jurisdictions, and goes to the areas where the crimes have been committed to make his or her own observations. A report can then be provided summarizing this information based on the analyst's research and analysis. This type of profiling information can help give investigators leads and is a useful item in the arsenal of tools used in a criminal investigation.

Intelligence Analysis

Intelligence analysis, at the present time, occurs more often at the state and federal levels. It focuses on organized crime, terrorism, and supporting specific investigations with information analysis and presentation. Analysts can support investigations by becoming the "processor" of information for officers. In a homicide investigation, the tools of analysis can be used to organize investigative information and display it in the form of time lines and association link charts. The utility of analysts in investigative support has not been realized by most local law enforcement agencies. This also is a likely area of future growth in crime analysis, as law enforcers conducting investigations realize the high value of well-crafted knowledge gleaned from information.

Crime analysis differs from intelligence analysis in another key area. Intelligence analysis usually starts with an identified problem statement or identified problem subject (such as motorcycle gangs), and information specific to the topic is then identified, gathered, analyzed, and disseminated. Crime analysis often involves the *discovery* of crime problems and the *identification* of the nature of crime problems by filtering through large quantities of data.

Operations Analysis

Operations analysis examines *how a law enforcement agency is using its resources.* It focuses on such topics as deployment, use of grant funds, redistricting assignments, and budget issues. In many agencies crime analysts are asked to assist on special projects for the department that fall into the category of operations analysis.

For example, when a city considers annexing additional land, the police department needs to determine several things:

- Current calls-for-service load (by whoever is currently servicing the area).
- Projected growth: type of growth (residential, commercial, entertainment, and so on) and projected population increase (day and night).
- Response times by current/proposed staffing.

- Recommended additional hires needed to provide same level of coverage/response currently provided to citizens.
- Any redistricting of current city property that may occur as a result of the annexation.

These are but a few of the issues that must be considered in annexing additional land into a police jurisdiction. A person conducting operations analysis will encounter these types of issues.

SUMMARY

Crime analysis is a growing field seeking to define itself. You, in the role of crime analyst, often have the power to chart the direction your law enforcement agency will take regarding the types of crime analysis it will conduct. In the current "state of the art," the emphasis is on automation of the traditional administrative crime analysis tasks—those involving statistical analysis of crime and calls-for-service data. Most agencies are transitioning to a tactical and strategic crime analysis focus, dedicated to helping patrol officers and investigators apprehend criminals as well as assisting in problem-oriented and community policing efforts. You may direct your agency toward this trend by producing useful tactical and/or strategic crime analysis products. As the information you produce helps officers and detectives do better police work, your agency likely will begin to realize the value of tactical and strategic crime analysis.

SUGGESTED READINGS

Gottlieb, S.L., Arenberg, S., and Singh, R. (1994). *Crime Analysis: From First Report to Final Arrest.* Montclair, CA: Alpha Publishing.

Heuer, R.J. (1999). *Psychology of Intelligence Analysis.* Center for the Study of Intelligence, Central Intelligence Agency. Available online: <http://www.cia.gov/csi/books/19104>.

Hutton, S.A. and Myrent, M. (1999). *Incident-Based Crime Analysis Manual: Utilizing Local-Level Incident Reports for Solving Crimes.* Chicago: Illinois Criminal Justice Information Authority.

Peterson, M. (1998). *Applications in Criminal Analysis: A Sourcebook.* Westport, CT: Greenwood Press.

Chapter 2

The Crime Analyst's Toolbox

OVERVIEW

The objective of this chapter is to give you an idea of what tools you will need to be a good crime analyst. The nuts and bolts of crime analysis are research and analytical skills. A crime analyst will read thousands, if not tens of thousands, of crime reports in a year. Being a quick yet careful reader is a definite asset. Having a good memory for significant details will be a tremendous plus. Curiosity is mandatory. Finding pleasure in discovering relationships among variables and the ability to uncover these relationships are also important assets for working in the field.

Crime analysis involves a multidisciplinary approach to looking at crime. Experienced analysts agree that innate analytical abilities are as critical to the crime analyst's job as analytical training. Crime analysis demands a repertoire of skills and abilities. Knowledge of a variety of computer software applications, basic to advanced statistics, computer mapping, public speaking, journalism, creative problem solving, logic, history, criminology, sociology, psychology, law, criminal justice—all are foundations for a good crime analyst. No one person can be an expert in so many areas, which is why some crime analysis units are staffed by analysts specializing in GIS (crime mapping) or statistics, as well as by generalists. Most agencies do not have the luxury of hiring specialists, so their analysts generalize, doing their best work in the area of their own expertise.

Dissemination of objective written reports is a crime analyst's main duty. Although there is some room for creativity in the work environment, reports must be factual and to the point. Officers do not want to read creative essays. The analyst must be able to gather and summarize useful information in a comprehensible format for the intended audience in a timely manner. Old information usually is not perceived as being useful in local law enforcement—current trends that can assist in real-world problem-solving efforts, as well as improve officer safety, are perceived as more valuable to most police officers.

To determine what information is important to a law enforcement agency, the individual assigned to analyze crime must have developed analytical skills. From all the reports and other information sources, he or she must be able to pull out relevant facts and interpret their meaning. The significance of the identified sets of facts must be articulated in a comprehensible manner.

Often individuals with no background in crime analysis are hired as the first crime analyst in their agency. Enthusiasm and self-motivation are needed for any crime analyst position, but are especially crucial in these circumstances. The new crime analyst must be willing to take risks, to say, "I don't know," and to be willing to make mistakes while working on the challenging task of developing a crime analysis function. Risk taking also involves standing up for what you think to be true, such as the likelihood of a serial offender committing another crime. Often, as noted in the Summary in Chapter 1, the first crime analysts in a law enforcement agency will have to educate that particular agency about the functions of crime analysis after researching the field themselves.

For those who do not already have well-developed computer skills, devoting time to learning a variety of software programs is mandatory. Computer skills are an absolute necessity for crime analysts. Even if a crime analyst is quite computer literate, his or her agency is likely to have unfamiliar software. The ability and desire to learn new skills are requirements. Crime analysis is a changing field—new tools are routinely developed. Open-mindedness about learning new things will be significant in determining how successful the crime analyst will be in his or her new position.

Desirable *qualities* in a crime analyst:

- Curiosity
- Self-motivation
- The ability to work independently
- Self-confidence

- Objectivity
- Diplomacy
- Risk-taking ability
- Determination
- Creativity
- Initiative
- Ability to admit *and* correct mistakes
- Desire to learn
- Open-mindedness

Skills a crime analyst will need to have and/or learn:

- Research skills
- Writing skills
- Pattern recognition skills
- Statistical analysis skills
- Computer literacy
- Time management skills
- Inference and critical thinking skills
- Public speaking/presentation skills
- Communication/interpersonal skills
- Group facilitation skills

The new crime analyst may have the potential to be a very good crime analyst, but lack the skills needed for success. Although the workplace may provide training opportunities, an individual employed as a crime analyst probably should choose to develop some of these skills on his or her own.

Local schools and community colleges offer classes on software applications. Studying database and spreadsheet applications is very useful. With the constant changes in computer technology there is always more to learn, and taking classes can help an analyst stay up todate. Employers will usually pay for or supplement the cost of these types of classes if funding is available.

If public speaking and presentations are difficult for an analyst, he or she may want to consider joining Toastmasters, an organization that helps individuals develop and polish public-speaking abilities. Public speaking courses are also offered by professional development trainers and at colleges.

Software exists in the form of tutorials in many subjects, including statistics. Investing in this type of educational tool may help the analyst in skill building. Such software allows individuals to learn at convenient times and places. Books on developing critical thinking skills are available in libraries.

This chapter provides information on some of the tools of crime analysis. It should be understood that these tools are merely described—it is up to the reader to learn the skills needed to become a well-rounded crime analyst. As technology changes and improves, new tools will become available. This chapter will touch upon just *some* of the knowledge and methods that prove helpful in analyzing crime.

EQUIPMENT

Anyone working in crime analysis should consider obtaining a computer with the following features:

- Maximum available central processing unit, memory, and hard drive capacity
- Maximum available size monitor (for viewing maps and large databases)
- A modem or Internet LAN connectivity
- A floppy disk drive, CD-ROM drive, and DVD drive
- External storage in the form of a Zip drive

Analysts need access to printers (preferably a color printer), to a plotter for large maps, desktop software such as MS Office or Corel, and mapping software such as ArcView or MapInfo. A scanner and a color photocopier are also major equipment assets for a crime analyst. Internet access is a necessity as well as e-mail and fax capabilities.

KNOWLEDGE OF THE LAW

If you are a new civilian crime analyst, you may have little or no law enforcement experience. If this is the case, it is necessary for you to study the penal codes of the jurisdiction in order to understand how crimes are classified. This usually means learning the numeric equivalent of a crime and the meaning of the criminal charge. For example, in New York, Penal Law 140.30 is a burglary first charge. This is the charge used in crimes considered to be home invasions, but it also includes certain domestic incidents classified as burglaries. Understanding the crime equivalents of penal codes is crucial.

You, the analyst, must understand how the information is captured on crime reports in the form of specific charges. Within those charges, you must filter out the types of crimes that are not part of a larger pattern or trend. For example, you may map burglaries within a jurisdiction and have what appears to be a geographic pattern, but if you have not read the reports or found a way to sort out the types of burglaries that involve domestic issues, suspicious reported thefts of such things as "rent-to-own" items, or events that are isolated and person-specific rather than serial in occurrence, you may not have a meaningful pattern at all. In fact, eliminating those reports may allow you to uncover a meaningful pattern elsewhere.

Thus, you must not only learn the law—you must learn to identify what is meaningful to analyze within the parameters of the law, and within the limits of the resources dedicated to crime analysis.

KNOWLEDGE OF INVESTIGATIVE PROCESSES

Since crime analysts often support investigators with information, you should learn as much as possible about investigative process in your agency. In the Las Vegas Police Department, crime analysts are encouraged to take the same inservice training as investigators in their area of specialty. Thus, for example, a crime analyst focusing on sex offenses would attend any training available for sex-crime investigators. You should take advantage of any such training opportunities if presented with opportunities to study investigative subjects, issues, and processes relevant to the crimes they analyze.

Frequent, ongoing communication with investigators will help you understand what information would be helpful to support investigations. It will help you to develop reports and bulletins that will be meaningful to those trying to solve criminal cases. Communication with investigators in other law enforcement agencies regarding similar crime series, patterns, and trends is also important.

The role of an investigator is to establish that a reported crime actually was committed, to identify and apprehend the suspect, to recover stolen property, and to assist the state in prosecuting the individual charged with an offense.

The role of the crime analyst in supporting investigations is apparent. You, as a crime analyst, can help the investigator by researching crimes by suspect and vehicle description, property stolen, MO factors, parole/probation information, field interview forms, and other data sources. This assistance can free investigators to do more fieldwork and thus enhance the probability of arrest.

Less apparent, but still important, is the fact that crime analysts may be more likely to increase the sharing of information between investigators within a police department, between law enforcement agencies, and cross-jurisdictionally, because they are not in competition with investigators trying to make a "good" arrest.

KNOWLEDGE OF MODERN POLICING STRATEGIES

Although a crime analyst's agency may not be utilizing all of the modern policing strategies listed in the following, it *is* important to be aware of current policing philosophies in order to share ideas with colleagues and to understand the best practices of other agencies. The most important reason to learn about these concepts is that *all* these strategies are predicated on the analysis of crime. A few resources to get you started in investigating these subjects in more depth are included at the end of this chapter.

Policing strategies to study:

- Problem-oriented policing
- Community-oriented policing
- COMPSTAT
- Intelligence-led policing

Problem-Oriented Policing

Problem-oriented policing approaches the root problems that cause crime and seeks to eliminate or reduce them. To implement problem-oriented policing, officers are often trained to use what is called the SARA model, developed by Herman Goldstein (1990). This model consists of *scanning* to identify a problem, *analysis* of the problem, *response* to the problem, and *assessment* of the efficacy of specific problem-solving strategies.

Crime analysts can contribute valuable information for problem-oriented policing efforts. Crime analysts can analyze information to verify whether the perceived problem actually is a problem as well as uncover significant problems that may not be apparent on the surface. Currently, crime analysts are an underutilized resource in problem-oriented policing.

To learn more about this concept, read Herman Goldstein's *Problem-Oriented Policing* (1990). The Police Executive Research Forum also promotes problem-oriented policing and hosts an annual conference on this topic. For more information visit the Police Executive Research Forum's Web site: <www.policeforum.org>.

Community-Oriented Policing

Community-oriented policing involves police partnerships with community members, working together to address crime and public disorder problems with the collective goal of preventing crime. In some agencies, crime analysts provide information to the community and are part of the collaboration process.

The U.S. Department of Justice's Community-Oriented Policing Services (COPS) office has a wealth of information about community-oriented policing at their Web site: <www.usdoj.gov/cops>.

COMPSTAT

The COMPSTAT process originated in the NYPD and is based on four principles:

- Accurate and timely intelligence
- Effective tactics
- Rapid deployment of personnel and resources
- Relentless follow-up and assessment

COMPSTAT (an acronym for computer statistics) functions separately from the crime analysis unit of the NYPD. It is a tool to hold police managers accountable for the crime in their respective jurisdictions. The NYPD has hosted annual COMPSTAT conferences for law enforcement personnel from outside agencies to view and learn about the process. A number of law enforcement agencies have adapted COMPSTAT to their police jurisdictions. In some agencies, crime analysis units were created to help develop information for COMPSTAT-type efforts.

The COMPSTAT process involves police management examination of crime-mapping data and other descriptive statistical data to note problem areas and specific crime problems and hold police staff accountable for addressing these uncovered issues. At group meetings, police managers must explain how they are working toward eliminating crime problems and, in some jurisdictions, are penalized if they do not demonstrate knowledge and implementation of strategies for their specific jurisdictions. For more information contact:

> Office of the Chief of the Department
> New York City Police Department
> 1 Police Plaza
> New York, NY 10038
> 212-374-6710

Intelligence-Led Policing

Intelligence-led policing is a concept in law enforcement that focuses on using intelligence products for decision making by police managers at the tactical and strategic level. The United Kingdom is implementing this concept at every level of policing. "Intelligence" in this case refers to the information provided by both crime and intelligence analysis. Intelligence, in this process, can be equated with actionable information. This trend in policing puts analysis of crime *and* intelligence information at the center of all police efforts. For more information visit the United Kingdom's National Criminal Intelligence Service (NCIS) Web site: <http://www.ncis.co.uk/ilp.html>.

These different policing strategies are not geographically or politically exclusive—all of them can be adapted and utilized in any police agency.

LINKAGE ANALYSIS

A major component of tactical crime analysis consists of linkage analysis, sometimes called "comparative case analysis." Linking crimes through determining similarities is the essence of crime series identification. A crime series is identified only when enough similarities exist to support the theory that the same person or persons perpetrated a set of crimes.

Some of the crimes most likely to occur in patterns and series include robberies, sexual offenses, burglaries, vehicle thefts and recoveries, and vehicle break-ins. Within those crimes are sets of crimes that the analyst can specifically target for attention.

When searching databases or crime reports for emerging series, an analyst can use systematic strategies to look for particular activities and facts that will help to locate emerging crime series earlier than in past policing practices, prior to systematic analysis. Most crimes can be analyzed temporally and geographically, but not all crimes in a crime series or pattern occur in a pattern of time or place. Studying crime by time of day, day of week, time of month, or season will help identify temporal patterns. Mapping crime will help identify geographic patterns of crime. However, neither can substitute for the careful reading of crime reports to uncover the less obvious links.

Linkage analysis charts and matrices are tools to organize facts in potential crime series and, when appropriate, to display such information for officers. Table 2.1 is an example of a matrix that can be used to evaluate links among crimes for series identification. This type of chart compares the variables within specific crime incidents to find which crimes have the most similarities. Variables with more significance can be weighted in this type of analysis. The following chart is a simple example of how a matrix may be used in an effort to link crimes. In this example, variables are not weighted.

It is possible to infer from this chart that Case 2 and Case 6 are related, and that Case 5 is also likely to be part of this rape series. In Cases 2 and 6

TABLE 2.1. Example of a Linkage Analysis Matrix

	Victim's hands duct-taped together	Victim burned with cigarette	Rapist wore red jacket	Rape took place in park	Victim was jogging in park before rape	Rape took place between 6-9 a.m.	Rapist was white male age 40-45
Case 1	X				X		unknown
Case 2		X	X	X	X	X	X
Case 3	X	X					
Case 4	X				X		X
Case 5		X	X		X		unknown
Case 6			X	X	X	X	X

the rapist was a white male, age forty to forty-five, wearing a red jacket. Those rapes occurred in parks between 6 and 9 a.m., and the victims were jogging in parks before the rapes. In Case 5, the rape did not occur in a park and the victim is unsure of the age of the rapist. However, she was burned with a cigarette during the rape (as was the victim in Case 2), had been jogging in a park immediately before the rape, and the suspect wore a red jacket. These similarities lead to an inference that the same suspect is involved as in Cases 2 and 6. It appears that Case 1 is unlikely to be related, since the only common variable to cases 2 and 6 is the fact the victim was jogging in the park before the rape. It can be concluded that Case 3 is not related because the race and age of the rapist differs from the suspect's race and age in Cases 2 and 6.

To find links in crime reports, look for similar variables. The more similarities, the likelier it is that crimes are related, but until we have proof that crimes are related, we must remember that we are only formulating hypotheses. A hypothesis truly is only an educated guess, but using scientific methodologies and critical thinking, the likelihood of being correct is significantly higher than less careful approaches to thinking about crime problems.

STATISTICAL ANALYSIS

Statistics are an important tool in the crime analyst's toolbox. A crime analyst applies principles of research, including statistical analysis, to aid law enforcers in discovering useful information to fight crime and maximize use of resources. Statistics help the analyst turn vast amounts of seemingly meaningless numbers into a picture of an event or series of events. There exists a vast array of statistical tools available to the crime analyst; however, in reality most CAs rely on only a handful of basic statistical tools. Since this is a book for beginners, only the basics are discussed. Most analysts are not advanced statisticians, but it is advantageous to learn as much as possible about this subject in order to understand the advances in the field, especially in statistical analysis related to crime mapping and forecasting.

Descriptive Statistics

Descriptive statistics are the primary statistical tool of the crime analyst. Descriptive statistics involve summarizing data into a format that provides a "descriptive" picture of an event or a series of events. Some examples of descriptive statistics include measures of central tendency, such as the average (mathematical center of a distribution of numbers), the median (the fiftieth percentile of a distribution), and the mode (the most frequent occurrence of a number in a distribution). Other descriptive techniques include measures of variability (range, variance, and standard deviation) and measures that define the relationship (association) between two or more data elements.

Inferential Statistics

Inferential statistics differ from descriptive statistics in several ways. First, and most important, inferential statistics are used for making inferences about a large population based upon data collected from a small subset of that population. Inferential statistics are probability based, that is, with only a small amount of information the analyst uses inferential statistics for making a "best guess" about some phenomenon occuring in the population. That "best guess" is based upon the probability that the subset you are working with is similar to the population as a whole.

Inferential statistics play a very small role in the day-to-day work of most crime analysts. Generally, it is not practical for a CA to draw a sample of data just to make a probability-based "best guess" about when or where the next crime is going to occur. Although inferential statistics are not always practical for the crime analyst, however, making inferences is a critical component of the CA responsibilities.

If you understand your data and your population you can use descriptive statistics to paint a picture of that population. If you have a descriptive picture of the population you can then make inferences about how that population will act.

Some inferential statistical techniques can be very useful as descriptive tools. However, it is important to understand that when you use these tools you are no longer using their probabilistic powers: you are using them as descriptive tools. The inferences you draw from these statistical tools apply only to the population of your jurisdiction. You cannot transfer inferences about the characteristics of these events to other jurisdictions or populations.

Common Uses of Statistics in Crime Analysis

Crime rates—the comparison of crimes reported in a population in a specific area over a period of time.

Clearance rates—the comparison of number of crimes cleared (by arrest or other means) to the number of crimes reported.

Crime-trend data—the percentage change in number (increase, decrease, or no change) of crimes in a crime category over a specified time period.

Forecasting—forecasting the occurrence of a crime based on statistical analysis of dates, times, and places in a crime series.

PROFILING

The origin of the word profile is the Italian word *profilare,* which, according to *Webster's Dictionary* (1987), translates as "to outline." In criminal investigations a profile is a form of outline speculating on characteristics of a particular criminal. The crime analyst at the local law enforcement level may not engage in the in-depth psychological profiling, but knowledge of profiling techniques and the availability of profiling resources can be helpful in efforts to analyze crime.

Behavioral and Psychological Profiling

Behavioral profiling and psychological profiling are methods of theorizing about a serial criminal's behavioral and psychological characteristics based on analysis of evidence from crimes committed and related facts. The hypotheses developed in this type of profiling can help investigators narrow their search for suspects. Some crime analysts are trained in this type of profiling methodology.

Behavioral and psychological profiling have been primarily used for serial murderers and rapists, but future research in this field should help crime analysts to address the challenge of identifying possible serial robbers and burglars as well.

Geographic Profiling

Geographic profiling is a specialized investigative tool developed by D. Kim Rossmo, formerly of the Vancouver Police Department, now director of research at the Police Foundation in Washington, DC. Geographic profiling is "an information strategy for serial crime investigation that analyzes crime site information to determine the most probable area of offender residence" (Rossmo 2000, 259). Serial murders and rapes are the most commonly geographically profiled crimes, but other serial crimes such as robberies and arsons may be profiled using this technique. The methodology of criminal geographic targeting (CGT) is based on a patented algorithm that produces information on the likelihood of an offender's residing within an area based on analysis of crime site coordinates and other investigative information (Rossmo 2000, 197).

Geographic profiling is not a hands-on tool available for crime analysts to use at this time. However, specially trained individuals are available to help investigators narrow their search for serial criminals by providing geographic profiling on a consult basis.

SPATIAL ANALYSIS

Spatial analysis involves analyzing crime as it occurs in space. All crimes have a location (even crimes in cyberspace involve the location of computers) and this fact makes analysis of crime location logical and reasonable. Geographic profiling is a specialized form of spatial analysis incorporating investigative and profiling knowledge. The development of Geographic Information Systems (GIS) software allows law enforcement agencies to study the geography of crime in unprecedented manners. Hot spots of crime indicated by visual clusters, density maps of crime, and statistical analysis of crime over time in space can be conducted using GIS. Geographic Information Systems (GIS) have brought crime analysis to the attention of many government agencies that had not before given crime analysis focused attention. Investment in the newest software and hardware, coupled with training and good data, make it possible for an increasing number of police departments to make their own crime maps fairly easily. Along with analysis of crime data, mapping can allow for analysis of other variables that may impact on crime.

Crime mapping and spatial analyses have become a focus of many crime analysis units and have introduced many local police agencies to the concept of systematic crime analysis. Chapter 4 discusses this type of analysis in greater detail and provides a number of resources to help you get started.

SUMMARY

The information a good crime analyst can provide to his or her agency is as much qualitative as quantitative. The former administrative focus on analyzing numbers and producing statistics has been supplanted with a much more comprehensive model of crime analysis. Practical information on the qualitative nature of specific crime series and patterns leads to the creation of more useful information tools for officers and detectives on the streets.

For example, the crime analyst notices a burglary hot spot on a map and notes that it is statistically significant after conducting the relevant calculations. He or she reads the related crime reports and finds that, although the numbers and the maps show a problem, the specific details of the crime show that the crimes are unrelated in that they have different MOs and different suspect descriptions. This means different policing strategies apply—looking for certain criminals will not solve the crime problem. Perhaps there are several known "drug houses" in the area, and some of the burglaries are committed by different addicts looking for quick cash. Arresting these burglars will not necessarily reduce the crime in this area. We may expect this to remain a burglary hot spot until the drug houses are eliminated. Quantitative and qualitative analysis are partners in the crime analyst's toolbox.

SUGGESTED READINGS

Goldstein, H. (1990). *Problem-Oriented Policing*. Philadelphia: Temple University.

McDonald, P. (2002). *Managing Police Operations: Implementing the NYPD Crime Control Model Using COMPSTAT*. Belmont, CA: Wadsworth.

Morgan, D.J. (1998). *The Thinker's Toolkit: 14 Powerful Techniques for Problem Solving*. New York: Times Business-Random House.

Rossmo, D.K. (2000). *Geographic Profiling*. Boca Raton, FL: CRC Press.

Smith, A. (Ed.) (1997). *Intelligence-Led Policing: International Perspectives on Policing in the 21st Century*. International Association of Law Enforcement Intelligence Analysts.

Spelman, W.G. (1987). *Beyond Bean Counting: New Approaches for Managing Crime Data*. Washington, DC: Police Executive Research Forum.

Chapter 3

Moving Through the Stages
of Crime Analysis

There are five generally recognized stages in crime analysis: collection, collation, analysis, dissemination, and feedback. Each stage
is important and no stage should be overlooked or disregarded since
failure to complete all five stages can result in inaccurate, incomplete,
or misleading conclusions. In this chapter, the five stages are ex-
plained in the context of performing tactical crime analysis; however,
these five stages can also be applied to any type of crime analysis.

COLLECTION

First, you, the analyst, must *collect* the data. Many sources of data
and information are available to analysts, although the most obvious
is probably the most important: police reports. Police reports include
crime incident reports, investigative follow-up reports, calls-for-
service records, and arrest reports. All available police reports in your
jurisdiction should be evaluated as potential information sources. Police reports may be your primary data source, but many other sources
can and should be tapped.

Other sources of data include field interview forms (FIFs) or field
interview reports (FIRs), probation and parole supervisors' reports,
U.S. census data (demographics), newspapers (and other media), the
Internet, other analysts, housing authorities, school officials, mall security guards, and hospital security. Business information, tax data,
land-use records, and neighborhood watch information are also worth
exploring. Anywhere you can obtain data or information regarding illegal events, suspicious subjects or circumstances, or about the gen-

eral geography of a given area—information that may be helpful in the fight against crime—is worth exploring.

Probably the most underutilized source of information is the knowledge of experienced detectives and officers. Many times these individuals possess a great deal of information on historical events involving the same "players," which they are more than willing to share, but have yet to be asked. Sometimes an analyst's best sources of information come from a one-hour lunch with a detective or a ride-along with a seasoned patrol officer. Their insights provide an analyst with specific information about certain offenders and also provide information about crime trends in particular areas (neighborhoods, districts, and so on) over the past five, ten, fifteen, twenty, or even twenty-five years. Often the dynamics of the changes these officers have experienced can provide an analyst with insights not available through any other source.

Analysts face a variety of problems and challenges concerning gathering data. First and foremost, what if data are not available? Since we must provide *timely and accurate information* to our customers, how do we address the fact that the records unit is three months behind in entering data? Or the issue that, on a regular basis, dozens of errors are on reports entered into the Records Management System (RMS)?

An analyst faced with this type of situation has many options. The first is to accept the fact that record entry is behind and current data for tactical analysis may not be available until the record unit is able to catch up. This is assuming the department is working from hand-written reports, transferring the basic information into a RMS for Uniform Crime Reports (UCR) or Incident-Based Reports (IBR) reporting. Rather, the analyst could focus the unit's efforts on strategic or administrative analysis. Although this is certainly an option, it is not the best one.

The new analyst may opt to focus on one to two (or more) specific crime types, requesting that as reports are turned into the records unit (before they go to the file cabinet marked "Reports to be entered") a copy is made and sent to the analyst for review. Let us say the analyst selects robbery and commercial burglary. Using the manual method of obtaining the police report information, an analyst can begin logging (manually or on a spreadsheet) the basic pertinent data from the police reports. Information such as report number, date, time, location, victim, suspect, vehicle, property, and MO can be captured and recorded for future analysis.

Another problem an analyst faces is consistency in reporting data. For instance, in a case involving items removed from the bed of a pickup truck, is it an auto burglary, theft from auto, or simple theft? Whatever the choice, it is important to be consistent in recording the data in the log, on the spreadsheet, or in the database. Different officers will report crime incidents in different formats, even though the same crime elements are present from report to report. It is important for analysts to recognize inconsistencies and attempt to correct them prior to the analysis.

A final problem commonly found in collecting data is in making the contacts necessary to gather the information. If the analyst does not know any probation or parole officers, school, hospital, or mall security, or does not know where to get U.S. Census data, it is imperative that the analyst pursue these avenues. Perhaps a co-worker (officer, detective, records clerk, or other) can steer the analyst toward these sources. Contact the sources by telephone or compose and send a letter introducing yourself and explaining your immediate and long-term goals. Explain how the information they possess is valuable to you, to the officers, and to the community. Develop network groups of people who can formally and informally share information. Remember, a simple telephone call from a parole officer advising you that Mr. Bad Guy, the robber who always targets fast-food restaurants, has been released from prison may be of interest to the assigned detective on the McDonald's robbery with a similar suspect description. Remember, a detective with no clues is often your best friend.

Know that no challenges related to data collection are insurmountable. It may not be easy, but it is possible to get the information needed to analyze crime. As long as the analyst keeps an open mind and is creative with his or her approach to collecting the data, the first stage of crime analysis will fall into place.

COLLATION

Collation involves organizing your information through categorization and, often, subcategorization. If the analyst is dealing with a stack of paper reports, field interview reports, or outside agency crime bulletins, the analyst's job is to sort them out. For instance, make a pile of residential burglary reports, a pile of robbery reports, a pile of auto thefts, and so on. Or, if using a database, the analyst may want to assign categories or field names to the reports, so that one simple query will bring up all the residential burglaries, robberies, or auto thefts. In more technologically advanced departments, categories can be assigned during the download from the Records Management System into the database by having the computer identify the statute, UCR code, or other unique value.

During the collation process, the analyst may have to "clean" the data—look for errors and correct them, or format the data to be compatible with the tools one uses for analysis. For example, if an analyst is going to computer-map locations, it is important and efficient to make sure the address fields are in a format compatible to automating the geocoding (locating address to point on map) process in the available software. Collation also allows one to properly categorize crimes for analysis, to look for those crimes that may have errors in reporting, or to add to incomplete reports by looking for more information.

Because the analyst has probably been given copies of everything from residential burglaries to civil matters to animal calls and traffic accidents, it is important for the analyst to determine what will be sorted. This can easily be determined based on three questions:

- How many reports are there?
- How much time do I have to devote to them?
- In which crime types do I have the best chance of identifying series/trends/patterns?

If 30,000 reports are submitted each year and only one analyst must collect and analyze all of them, it is obvious that only certain crime types will have to be selected for analysis. Perhaps, in this case, as with most new analysis units, the crime types chosen will be residential and commercial burglary, auto burglary, auto theft, robbery, and sex crimes. If the sheer number of just these types of reports make analysis of all of these prohibitive, the analyst may want to analyze just two or three crime types, such as robbery, sex offenses, and residential burglary. Focus on the crimes that occur in patterns in your district; if you are not certain what those crimes may be, ask experienced officers. The analyst may realistically have time to thoroughly read and review only twenty to twenty-five reports a day after all the other assigned duties are figured into the day. This, of course, depends on the length and depth of the reports the analyst receives, as well as the other duties the analyst is assigned. Whatever the case, after the analyst collects the data, he or she must next sort it into smaller, more manageable stacks, records, or databases so that the next step, analysis, can take place.

ANALYSIS

This is the heart of it all—analyzing the data collected and turning it into timely, useful, and accurate information for dissemination. The objective of analysis is to turn data into actionable information on crime series, patterns, and trends. It is your job to help the patrol officers, detectives, and command staff interpret the vast amount of data collected and collated to meet their primary objective: to reduce crime.

You must understand that this stage cannot be properly done unless the first two stages are completed. No one should try to skip to this stage without first collecting and collating the data. Often, analysts collect the data and try to skip right to analyzing it. Although in some situations it can be done this way, one would be very concerned about the amount of time that was spent trying to sift through all the sources, gathering data from each, as well as the quality of the output. How many information sources were omitted by skipping the collation stage? After analyzing this possibly incomplete data, the analyst may prepare an inaccurate (based on data) forecast for the sworn officers. Without collating the data, the analyst will find great difficulty in effectively analyzing the data.

As an example of the analysis process, we will discuss analyzing the MO of crime. Analyzing MO factors using linkage analysis involves searching files (automated and manual) to determine if offenses are related (i.e., a crime series is occurring) by looking at similarities in the offender's actions and descriptions of the crime. Keep in mind that there are a number of approaches to analyzing crime and this is only one example.

For example, out of twelve reported commercial burglaries in the past month, perhaps seven have occurred on Saturday nights between 9 p.m. and 11:30 p.m., all with smashed front windows and all at sports clothing stores. Linkage analysis bases the crime series on the fact that the windows were smashed and sports clothing stores were targeted. Statistical analysis would be used to measure the frequency of the crimes and time periods of occurrences. Spatial analysis involves looking at the locations on maps to see the spatial relationships of each crime occurrence.

Analysis also is conducted on the data to assist in *identifying suspects*. Although there are certainly many "known offenders" in every community, cities grow and change, and taking into consideration the high mobility of virtually every single person, law enforcement agencies must continually assess *who is doing what,* especially looking for the most active criminals in the community. While conducting analysis, the analyst should be able to review previous cases in which suspects have been identified, searching for reports with similar MOs so that suspect correlation can take place. In other words, in keeping with our previous example of commercial smash-and-grabs, the analyst would search history or known-offender files for information on known commercial burglars whose MO was to smash the front windows of sports clothing stores.

Analysis is also used for *matching cases* (suspect-crime correlation). Once an arrest has been made and the MO of the offender has been identified, the analyst can research all similar incidents for which the offender may be responsible. Searching into history files to find commercial burglaries in which the point of entry was a front window can help link crimes in a series such as the previous example. Criminals can be charged with more crimes that they committed if links can be found through analysis and evidence collected by officers. Career criminals can then be prosecuted for their offenses and serve time in jail, the consequence of their criminal behavior.

Another use for analysis is *target/victim profiling.* Again, using our previous example of commercial burglaries, an analyst can readily see that not only are the known victim stores targets for the suspect(s) but also other sports clothing stores in the area, keeping in mind that geographical boundaries such as city or county lines are not recognized by crooks. Using this information, a crime analyst can (and should) work with the department's crime prevention unit or patrol officers to make contact with possible future targets. Those possible targets should be contacted and advised of the situation. Additional crime prevention measures within reason (such as laminating glass, adding security guards, checking the alarm system, and so on) can then be taken to help deter, detect, or delay the targets from becoming the next victim.

We cannot forget *forecasting*. It certainly would be outstanding if an analyst could take a crime series, develop an accurate forecast (i.e., predict the date, time, and location of the next hit—providing the suspect's name and vehicle description would be even better), and catch the bad guys every single time. In reality, it does not happen that way. Analysts are often faced with a crime series where, intuitively, they know all of the incidents are related. Perhaps the first robbery incident occurred on a Sunday morning at 3:30, at a gas station near a highway, and the suspect was described as an unknown male wearing a black ski mask, white T-shirt, and jeans and brandishing a silver gun. Two weeks later, a robbery occurs at a convenience store at 2 a.m. near a major thoroughfare, with a masked male wearing a T-shirt and jeans, revealing a silver handgun. Two days after that, yet another robbery with the same suspect description occurs at a gas station across the street from the police station at 4 a.m.

How can any prediction be made based on time/date analysis with such an erratic robbery suspect? Some conclusions can be drawn, however, that may assist patrol officers and/or detectives to at least narrow the time frame and target locations that may be hit next. For example, common sense tells the analyst that this is a midnight shift concern. Other than general distribution of the crime series information, extra or directed patrol at convenience stores and gas stations does not need to take place on the day or evening shifts. Rather, the analyst should identify those gas stations and convenience stores open all night (twenty-four-hour businesses), especially those near major thoroughfares and highways. Using crime prevention officers, community-oriented policing officers, and midnight patrol officers, the businesses can be contacted, advised of the current crime series, and provided advice on what to do if they feel they are being targeted or if they fall victim to a robbery. Furthermore, patrol officers can provide the identified possible targets with extra patrol as duty permits.

Three weeks pass with no more incidents. What has happened to the suspect? Was the analyst wrong? Were the incidents actually random? Although it is certainly possible that the three incidents were committed by three different suspects, it is equally likely that the extra patrols for the businesses, media attention provided concerning the incidents, or other crime prevention efforts may have run the suspect out of the area, or at least temporarily put him on guard and out of (the robbery) business. Whatever the case, the efforts have paid off and the crime series has stopped, which is one of the main goals for crime analysts—to assist in preventing crime and to provide the citizens and businesses with a safer community.

Forecasting crime *is* possible. There are good statistical models for predicting crime, and crime analysts should implement these techniques whenever appropriate. The more crimes identified in a series, the more probable that the forecast will be accurate.

DISSEMINATION

Now that the information has been collected, collated, and analyzed where does this "timely, accurate, and useful" information go? It goes to the customer—that is, primarily to patrol officers, investigators, and command staff. In some police agencies, crime analysis information is available to the media, citizens, other city/government employees, and other law enforcement agencies. Departmental policies will determine who gets the information crime analysis produces.

One of the first and most prominent ways of disseminating the information is through various types of crime bulletins—this includes tactical, strategic, and administrative bulletins and reports.

The analyst and users should decide together what types, how many, and how often bulletins will be created and disseminated. Once the bulletins are created, they should be disseminated to the targeted audience. For instance, a tactical crime bulletin concerning the series of commercial burglaries would be passed on to the patrol officers, detectives, crime prevention officers, and other local jurisdictions. It may also be appropriate to disseminate the bulletin to the command staff, especially if the agency is using COMPSTAT or any other management accountability strategy.

Information may be disseminated by physically placing a copy in each officer's box, through interdepartmental mail, through a department's intranet e-mail, by fax, or by simply placing it on a bulletin board in or near the roll call room. Initially, the analyst may distribute a copy to every officer by physically placing the bulletin in each mailbox, but later discover that dissemination through the department's e-mail system may be a much more sensible idea, thus saving a large amount of paper and time. If the department does not yet have interdepartmental e-mail or an intranet, manually placing the bulletins in mailboxes may be the best idea.

After internal distribution is complete, the analyst should address external distribution. Until regional/statewide databases are readily available, one of the primary ways of exchanging information continues to be through cross-jurisdictional distribution of crime bulletins and monthly crime meetings between jurisdictions. The crime analyst's management staff *must* give permission to share such information prior to external dissemination. A fax network is a great way to distribute the bulletins in a timely manner.

It is possible to securely send crime bulletin information over the Internet via secure intranets, but these are not widely available. Although it certainly is possible with current technology to send documents with passwords over the Internet, it is known that hackers can easily break these codes and access the information. As more secure methods of disseminating information via the World Wide Web become more readily available, analysts will be able to take advantage of technology in this fashion, placing the bulletins on a secure site for police-only access.

The FBI has a secure intranet network for information sharing called Law Enforcement Online (LEO). Other such networks exist through the federally funded Regional Information Sharing Systems (RISS). More information on RISS and LEO can be found later in this book.

Whatever internal and external methods are chosen, keep in mind that the primary goal of crime analysis is to take collected, collated, and analyzed information and provide that information in a clear, understandable format to the targeted audience. Crime analysis is of no value if it does not provide information that is meaningful and useful in combating crime.

FEEDBACK AND EVALUATION

The final step is probably the most neglected. One of the most important aspects of being a *good* crime analyst is having the knowledge that the customers are using the products, reports, and information created. What is the fastest way to determine whether the crime analysis products are being used? Stop producing them. If individuals ask for the discontinued product, it might indicate that the product is being used. Keep in mind, however, that one reason for contacting and asking about a report might be just because, "I've always gotten it," which still does not address the question of whether the information is being used.

An efficient way of receiving feedback is to attach a short evaluation form to the final product. Obviously, if the information were being disseminated over e-mail, the form would have to be automated. Either way, the analyst should realize that probably less than half of the customers will take the time to complete an evaluation form. These forms should *not* be attached or included with every single product. If the customer is overburdened with having to fill out an evaluation form for each product, the analyst may find that the customers may stop asking (or at least ask much less frequently) for products, knowing that they are going to have to complete additional paperwork each time a request from crime analysis is made.

A major part of an analyst's feedback is going to come from informal methods of evaluating. Often, chance encounters with officers, investigators, or command staff will net a great interaction and some of the best feedback on a crime analysis product. The customer may have suggestions for changes that have not been relayed to the analyst for any number of reasons (did not have a chance, do not know how to use e-mail, did not know the analyst cared, and so on).

Other times, a response on a formal feedback form may spark an idea for a major (or not so major) positive change for future reports. Simply seeing another agency's report with similar information may provide the analyst with numerous ideas to improve current products.

How do we get feedback for the overall operation of the crime analysis unit? Certainly crime analysis units do not have one particular format of operations. Just as patrol officers set their own agendas for the day, keeping in mind the rules, regulations, and expectations set forth by their commanders, so do crime analysts. However, just as another employee can often think of a more efficient or more effective way of performing certain police or investigations functions, so, too, can those outside of the crime analysis unit think of improvements that can be made within a crime analysis unit.

A major way of receiving this type of evaluation is to randomly select officers, investigators, and command staff throughout the department (or division, if the unit is decentralized) and to set up numerous informal/formal meetings over the course of several weeks. During these meetings, which should be considered an "open forum," a general outline of the issues to be addressed should be provided to the group. The analyst initially should take lead in the meeting, explaining that the primary focus of the meeting is to improve the products and interactions between the sworn officers and the crime analysis unit staff. Several topics that can be discussed include:

- Availability of Crime Analysis Unit (CAU) staff: Does the staff attend roll calls? Does the staff take advantage of ride-along opportunities? Are the staff hours appropriate for the customers?
- Timeliness of disseminated products
- Usefulness of disseminated products
- Accuracy of disseminated products
- Officer's knowledge of CAU products
- Officer's knowledge of CAU capabilities
- Officer's knowledge of the location of archived CAU information

Once these issues have been appropriately addressed, a general discussion concerning the operation and function of the CAU can take place. In addition, suggestions for general improvements can be made at this time. Such examples include changing areas of responsibilities. Perhaps it would be more practical to have the analysts' responsibilities divided by geographic region, or by crime types (persons versus property versus financial crimes versus high-tech crimes) or by crime analysis type (tactical, strategic, or administrative). These issues, and any other pertinent to the group, can be addressed and discussed, and recommendations for change can be made.

Whatever the feedback (positive or negative) or how often it is received (daily or yearly), an effective crime analyst will keep in mind that the targeted audience (that is, the police officer, the command staff, the citizens, the media, other agencies, other intracity departments, and so on) is also the customer. Keeping the customer happy or at least content is a primary goal of nearly every effective organization in the world. If an analyst wants to be considered professional and intelligent, and if the analyst wants the unit to be known as an important part of the organization, taking into consideration the targeted audience's comments, suggestions, and feedback will play a major role in developing a highly respected crime analysis unit.

THE INTELLIGENCE CYCLE: ANOTHER VIEW OF THE STAGES OF ANALYSIS

With the major emphasis on Homeland Security issues, crime analysts should be aware of another view of the stages of analysis; The Intelligence Cycle, as used by the CIA and other intelligence analysts working in federal government.

The first stage of The Intelligence Cycle is *planning and direction.* Guidance from officials, identification of data to be collected, and identification of desired product outcome are part of this first stage.

The second stage is *collection.* As in the stages of crime analysis, collection involves raw information from whatever sources available. Because of the national scope, data may include satellite photography and secret sources of information. In The Intelligence Cycle this information is processed into finished intelligence.

The third stage is *processing.* Processing may involve language translations, decryption, and filtering through data.

The fourth stage is *all source analysis and production.* This stage involves converting intelligence information into an intelligence product.

The fifth stage of The Intelligence Cycle is *dissemination.* The intelligence product is distributed to the officials, which results in returning to stage one of the ongoing process.

SUMMARY

The stages of crime and intelligence analysis are best understood as a process that is cyclical rather than linear. During the process the analyst often must backtrack to clarify management needs for information, to collect more material, to collate into more subcategories, to analyze with a variety of different tools, or to develop different reports based on specific requests. Since new crimes happen every day, they need to be added to the ongoing collation and incorporated into the bigger picture. When done effectively, this interesting and challenging work allows you, the crime analyst, to help police officers do a better job in making communities safer.

Chapter 4

Geographic Information Systems: Issues and Resources

OVERVIEW

Some beginning crime analysts may have been hired solely for their geographic information systems (GIS) background. However, it is important to remember that spatial analysis is only one tool in crime analysis. Geographic Information Systems have brought crime analysis to the attention of many government agencies that had not given crime analysis focused attention before. Investment in the newest software and hardware, coupled with training and good data, makes it possible for more and more police departments to fairly easily make their own crime maps. Along with analysis of crime data, mapping can allow for analysis of other variables that may affect crime. This chapter will explore this type of analysis and discuss some of the pitfalls of crime mapping, as well as other issues to consider.

You will *not* learn how to map crime in this chapter, but you will become aware of some important aspects in analyzing crime using GIS. A list of GIS-related software developed by the Crime Mapping Research Center may be found at an Internet site listed at the end of this chapter, along with links to a user's group study from the Police Foundation. This combined information can guide you in selecting mapping software for your agency.

If your department is just starting out in computer crime mapping, it is recommended that you contact other agencies that have achieved a level of expertise in this area for recommendations on implementation. Some law enforcement agencies are part of larger, regional crime-mapping efforts. Regional crime mapping is very useful in strategic and trend analysis, but unless the data is in real time, it will not be effective for the tactical crime analysis needs of a local law enforcement agency. Crime analysts at the local level will benefit from having their own mapping capabilities in order to research their specific crime problems in a manner customized for their needs.

Be aware that your agency may be able to access geocoded data and technical support from your city's GIS program (if your city has GIS) and this can be an extremely valuable resource. Most law enforcement agencies with successful crime-mapping programs use the same software used by their respective city.

In the winter 2000 issue of *Crime Mapping News,* Colonel Ken Hughes from the Jefferson Parish Sheriff's Office enumerated some key points to consider when implementing a GIS program in your law enforcement agency as follows:

- GIS must be flexible to adapt to the evolving needs of an agency.
- GIS should be kept simple enough for police officers to use.
- Preformatted maps and reports should be established to increase the use and effectiveness of GIS within the police organization.
- GIS should be linked directly to the Records Management System to assist in investigations and operational needs.
- Updates must be done systemwide.
- GIS should support a Web application for information dissemination and to gain community support.
- Timely data is needed and necessary.
- Training and user support should be available continually.

POINTS TO REMEMBER WHEN CREATING CRIME MAPS

A single map is but one of an infinitely large number of maps that might be produced for the same situation or from the same data. (Monmonier 1996, 2)

What does this mean? It means that in the map-making process you have a number of choices to make which will affect how data is interpreted. A map is only a two-dimensional representation of a complex world, and what is selected to be displayed on a map requires some responsible thinking beforehand. Some things to consider:

- The size of symbols can minimize or exaggerate a problem—use care when choosing symbol size.
- The colors you select for various map features have emotional overtones. For example, red may be associated with blood and is more dramatic than another color. Too many different colors make it difficult for map readers, so limit yourself to no more than six colors when possible.
- Map readers may be color blind—be aware of that possibility and make maps that will convert to gray tones if necessary. Gray tones are also preferable for those lacking color printers.
- If you change the size of a map that is in .bmp or .jpg format, be aware that the scale bar does not adjust and thus will be inaccurate.
- Pictorial point symbols, such as guns for shootings, or automobiles representing vehicle thefts, can help get your information across more effectively.
- As the field of crime analysis moves toward becoming a true profession, we may want to develop standardized point symbols, as other professions have done. For example, we could decide that circles equal robberies, stars equal burglaries, and triangles equal sexual offenses. In this manner, maps would have a common symbol language for easier interpretation of information across departmental and jurisdictional boundaries.
- Maps can easily reflect bias, either intentionally or unconsciously. Try to remain objective and make every attempt to portray your information in a manner that does not reflect personal opinion.
- A map is only as good as the data you use. If you are getting a 70 percent success rate (or less) on geocoding incident locations from your data, you are not giving a clear picture of crime problems. Strive for high-quality data at the data entry point. Know your jurisdiction so that you make accurate geocoding choices. Geocode to the highest level possible.
- Experiment with data for a variety of levels of aggregation, and carefully qualify all conclusions (Monmonier 1996).
- Public presentation of crime data using maps requires special foresight. The audience often is not educated in spatial analysis and the interpretation of specific maps should accompany any maps presented (Harries 1999, 87).

- Do not map too many crimes on one map—the significance of specific crimes is lost if the map is too busy. Experiment with data and select crimes that might be related to one another, such as shooting, gun possession, and drug arrests.
- Mapping crime has become the focus of many crime analysis units, but the production of maps should never replace the analysis of the data on the map.

MAPPING OTHER DATA WITH CRIME DATA FOR ANALYSIS

Since crime does not occur in a vacuum and there are many factors influencing its occurrence and many other variables that exist in relation to crime, it is very useful to map other data along with crime data for in-depth analysis. Maps can help us uncover relationships we did not consider before.

Carolyn Rebecca Block and Lynn A. Green (1994), in their work *The Geoarchive Handbook: A Guide for Developing a Geographic Database As an Information Foundation for Community Policing,* list the following data sets as being useful to map for comparative analysis.

Law enforcement data
- Reported crime incidents
- Arrests
- Offender data
- Victim data
- Calls for service
- Probation release
- Corrections release
- Street-gang territories
- Recovery of property
- Nuisance addresses
- Criminal justice jurisdiction areas

Community data
- Street map data
- Property information
- Liquor-license locations
- Public transportation

- Schools
- Community organizations
- City parks
- Fire departments and police stations
- Public housing
- Population information
- Public health data
- Cognitive maps (public perception of neighborhoods or trouble spots)

Examples of maps that may help in tactical crime analysis:

- Robberies mapped with convenience-store and/or ATM locations
- Vehicle break-ins mapped near schools
- Sexual offenses mapped with registered sex offenders' addresses
- Assaults mapped with liquor-licensed establishments

Mapping crime with other data sets can be a definite asset and tool for a crime analyst. Use both creativity and common sense to map relevant data for your crime analysis needs.

PRIVACY ISSUES

While some law enforcement agencies display crime maps on the Internet for the world to view, others carefully guard crime maps and do not even share them outside the walls of the police department. Issues of accessibility of information to the public versus privacy of victims are not resolved in any universal manner (Casady 1999). Be sure to follow your agency's guidelines regarding dissemination of maps to other agencies and to the public.

Best Internet Examples of Crime Mapping in Local Law Enforcement

- <http://12.17.79.6/>
  Chicago Police Department's Citizen ICAM (Information Collection for Automated Mapping) Citizen ICAM allows the public to query the Chicago Police Department's database of reported

crime. The information on this Web page is also accessible through the Chicago Police Department's Records Division.

- <http://www.ci.lincoln.ne.us/city/police/>
  Lincoln Police Department, Nebraska
  Interactive crime map, maps, and tabular data.
- <http://www.ci.longmont.co.us/Police/crimeupdate/map.htm>
  Longmont Police Department, Colorado
  Updated weekly, the interactive city crime map displays the occurrences of serious crime throughout the city.
- <http://www.portlandpolicebureau.com/crimemapper.html>
  Portland Police Department, Oregon
  CrimeMapper interactive crime mapping and detailed graphs and reports that display crime data by month, day of week, and time of day.
- <http://www.ci.mesa.az.us/police/crime_analysis/patrol.htm>
  Mesa Police Department, Arizona
  Calls-for-service and crime maps.
- <http://www.ci.mesa.az.us/police/crime_analysis/maps/mapsmain.asp>
  City of Port Lucie Police Department, Florida
  Crime stats updated daily, searchable on the Web, monthly maps.
- <http://www.sannet.gov/police/stats/index.shtml>
  San Diego County, Automated Regional Justice Information System (ARJIS)
  Crime statistics and maps.
- <http://city.oakcc.com/maproom/crimewatch/>
  City of Oakland Police Department, California
  Crime Watch interactive mapping.
- <http://www.ci.boulder.co.us/police/crime/crime_map_flash.htm>
  City of Boulder Police Department, Colorado
  Weekly crime map.
- <http://www.new-orleans.la.us/cnoweb/nopd/maps/basecrimemap.html>
  City of New Orleans Police Department, Louisiana
  Crime maps.
- <http://www.sanantonio.gov/sapd/maps.asp?res=800&ver=true>
  San Antonio Police Department, Texas
  Crime data and maps.

RESOURCES FOR CRIME MAPPING

Crime Mapping & Analysis Program
National Law Enforcement & Corrections Technology Center
2050 East Iliff Avenue
Denver, CO 80208
Noah Fritz, Director
303-871-7458
<http:/www.nlectc.org/cmap/>

Introductory and advanced training through the Crime Mapping and Analysis Program is tuition-free; however, attendees must pay for their own transportation, food, and lodging. The cost is waived by applying for a tuition award as part of the application process. There may be a fee for obtaining your local base map. Both ArcView and MapInfo classes are offered. This agency offers links to many crime-mapping software products <http://www.ojp.usdoj.gov/cmrc/software/welcome.html>.

Carolinas Institute for Community Policing
1750 Shopton Road
Charlotte, NC 28217
704-336-8549
Toll Free Number: 1-877-726-0555
704-336-8449 Fax
info@cicp.org

This program, sponsored by the U.S. Department of Justice, offers courses in GIS for crime analysis and community policing.

Police Foundation
Computer Mapping Laboratory
1202 Connecticut Avenue NW
Suite 200
Washington, DC 20036
202-721-9777
202-659-9149 Fax
<www.policefoundation.org>
<pfmaplab@policefoundation.org>

This is a laboratory in the Research Division of the Police Foundation that is working on a variety of projects, including the provision of technical support to COPS grantees. Online resources at <http://www.policefoundation.org> include:

- *Crime Mapping News,* a quarterly newsletter for GIS, crime mapping, and policing.
- Crime analysis and crime mapping information clearinghouse
- Crime analysis and mapping product templates
- Frequently asked questions of crime analysis and mapping
- Geocoding in law enforcement
- Guidelines to implement and evaluate crime analysis and mapping in law enforcement
- *Manual of Crime Analysis Map Production*
- *Introductory Guide to Crime Analysis and Mapping*
- *Users' Guide to Mapping Software for Police Agencies*

Jerry Ratcliffe's homepage offers a great deal of information on crime mapping.
<http://jratcliffe.net/index.html>

National Guard Bureau Counterdrug Directorate's Digital Mapping Initiative (DMI)
<http://www-cddmi.forscom.army.mil>
<dmi@cddmi.forscom.army.mil>
404-363-5342
404-363-5342 Fax

Since 1993, this agency has provided free computer-generated maps to any law enforcement agency or DOD agency that supports counterdrug missions.

Other Crime-Mapping Training Links

- <www.esri.com/events>
  ESRI (makers of ArcView)
- <www.mapinfo.com/government>
  MapInfo Corporation
- <www.geospatialtech.com>
  GeoSpatial Technologies
- <www.ecricanada.com>
  ECRI (Geographic Profiling)

SUGGESTED READINGS

Block, C.R., Dabdoub, M., and Fregly, S. (1995). *Crime Analysis Through Computer Mapping*. Washington, DC: Police Executive Research Forum.

Harries, K. (1999). *Mapping Crime: Principle and Practice*. Washington, DC: U.S. Department of Justice.

La Vigne, N.G. and Wartell, J. (Eds.) (1998). *Crime Mapping Case Studies: Successes in the Field* (Volume 1). Washington, DC: Police Executive Research Forum.

La Vigne, N.G. and Wartell, J. (Eds.) (2000). *Crime Mapping Case Studies: Successes in the Field* (Volume 2). Washington, DC: Police Executive Research Forum.

Monmonier, M. (1996). *How to Lie with Maps*. Chicago: The University of Chicago Press.

Chapter 5

Crime Analysis Products

Crime analysis "products" include tactical crime analysis bulletins, administrative reports, and crime maps in a variety of formats. This chapter provides information on how to produce tactical crime analysis bulletins and describes administrative crime analysis products. Intelligence analysts produce a number of other products, which are listed and briefly described. Methods for evaluating the usefulness of your crime analysis products are suggested. The chapter concludes by discussing the concept of "analysis" in relation to "products." Examples of some crime analysis products are found in the appendix of this book

CREATING BULLETINS
FOR TACTICAL CRIME ANALYSIS

Although there certainly is *not* one correct way to write, publish, and distribute a crime bulletin, many guidelines can be followed to assist a new analyst in creating bulletins or to aid an analyst wishing to make changes to their department's daily, weekly, bi-weekly, or monthly bulletin.

From daily tactical bulletins to annual administrative reports, there are many types of publications that a crime analysis unit is expected to prepare for a variety of audiences. The focus here will be on tactical daily/weekly crime bulletins—those bulletins designed to assist patrol officers and investigators in identifying current crime series and most-active criminals.

How Does an Analyst Decide How Often to Publish?

Just because an agency is small does not mean that a bulletin cannot be published daily or just because an agency is big does not mean a bulletin should be published daily. An analyst should look at several factors when making the decision on how often a bulletin can/should be produced:

- How much time can the analyst devote to each bulletin?
- Will the officers (or targeted audience) be able to absorb the amount of information the analyst is proposing to disseminate?
- Does the analyst have enough valuable data/information to fill the bulletins for the frequency that is being considered?
- Who will publish the bulletins in the absence of the analyst?
- Will there be various types of bulletins (persons, property, arrests, warrants, and so on) or simply one bulletin containing all information?

The type and amount of activity occurring in a given jurisdiction may drive the number of tactical bulletins. Also, as new developments occur (additional crimes, suspects developed, and so on), the analyst may choose to update the information by publishing additional bulletins between "regular" publications. For example, if a series of residential burglaries was mentioned in a routine property crime report, but later develops into a major ordeal, the analyst may choose to publish a "Crime Series Memo" or other all-points bulletin.

A general guideline is to start with a weekly or biweekly bulletin, increasing the frequency of the bulletins slowly and cautiously as needed. If the analyst realizes he or she is overwhelming the officers with too much information, reduce the frequency of the bulletins or the content in each bulletin.

In What Computer Program Should the Document Be Prepared?

The simple answer here is "whatever program you have available." Whether the document is created in Word, WordPerfect, e-mail, or on a typewriter, the content of the document is what matters. If all that is available is a typewriter, copier, and some glue, use these items to produce the best possible bulletin. As more advanced technology becomes available to the analyst, the quality and the appearance of the bulletin can improve, but remember . . . it is all about the content.

What Types of Bulletins Will Be Published?

As mentioned previously, an analyst may decide to publish general interest bulletins if he or she is responsible for disseminating all crime analysis information. The frequency of the bulletins will depend on the amount of time, data, and other resources the analyst has to devote to the analysis, preparation, and dissemination of information. What format the information is published in is really up to the analyst and his or her supervisor. To decide the types of bulletins to be published, consider the following:

> How often will the publication be created/disseminated?
> Who is the targeted audience?
> What will the bulletin contain?
> * Persons crime information
> * Property crime information
> * Arrest information
> * Warrant information
> * Probation/parole information
> * Most-active criminals information
> * Most-wanted persons information
> * Stolen auto information
> * Crime series/crime trend information
> * Suspicious activity reports
> * Crime info sheets
> Will the analyst be able to address more than one of these topics in each bulletin?
> Where does the information come from and how timely is the information?

Keeping in mind the number of bulletins the analyst chooses to publish and the frequency of these bulletins, the previously listed types of information can be combined into the number of bulletins the analyst chooses to publish.

What Types of Information Should Be Included in the Bulletins?

The key to answering this question is for the analyst to first ask himself or herself the following question before placing *any* information, data, chart, graph, photo, or map in a bulletin for dissemination:

Does this information have intelligence value for the targeted audience? If the answer is "No" or "I don't know," the analyst may want to reconsider placing that information in the bulletin. Regardless of the answer, an analyst should refrain from putting the following in crime bulletins:

- Cartoons
- Misspelled words; bad grammar
- Inside jokes
- Rumors
- Insults (put-downs)
- Unconfirmed/unreliable information
- Personal opinions

Now that what should *not* be in bulletins has been established, an analyst should decided what *will* be in the bulletin.

Rapes, robberies, and burglaries are the easiest and most common types of incidents to track and are usually included in tactical bulletins. Other incidents such as ambulance calls, civil matters, and animal calls rarely would appear in a crime bulletin.

The following is a list of ideas for crime bulletins. This is *not* a comprehensive list, but simply a guideline to assist an analyst in preparing bulletins:

Summary of Police Reports:

- Keep it very simple (two to three sentences for most reports, four to five for major reports).
- Use complete sentences.
- Addresses, suspect names and vehicles, dates, and business names may be put in bold for emphasis.
- Do not include the victim's name unless it is pertinent to the report (i.e., who the person is changes the report's perspective— mental patient, repeat victim, and so on).
- Do not include personal opinions in the narrative.

For example:

- *Right:* ABC Company employees advised a w/m, 25-30, 6'0, 270, blk, bro, mustache, driving an older-model red Toyota two-door was observed in the area during the incident time frame. The vehicle has been observed in the area on numerous previous occasions and may be related to the incident.

- *Wrong:* Some ABC Company employees (who are questionable themselves) observed a trashy red Toyota two-door in the area and believe it is related to the incident because they see it in the area all the time.

Be sure to include the police report number, field interview sequence number, or other reference number for all reports. Include the name of the officer(s) who took the report and provide the name and phone number of the detective assigned to the report. *Note:* Including the officers' and detectives' names has an added benefit. People like to see their names in print (when in a positive light). This will help increase your readership.

Maps

- Should depict current activity
- Focus on hot spots, crime series, and current events
- Should be clear, easy to read, and appropriately sized for bulletin
- Major streets/landmarks should be labeled
- Should include title, north arrow, legend, scale, and date
- Should have symbols large/clear enough to be read when printed
- Should not be based on colors (if copies will be in black and white)

Charts/Graphs

- Limit charts and graphs; use them wisely and sparingly.
- Some ideas include incident month-to-month or year-to-year comparisons.
- Make sure the charts are clearly labeled and require little to no explanation; they should speak for themselves.

Pictures

- Officers love pictures
- Arrested, wanted, active: put those suspect/arrestee pictures in there.

- *Note:* Save pictures as .jpg rather than .bmp whenever possible; they use up much less "space" when sending bulletins through e-mail or over the Internet.

Outside Agency Information

Especially as the trend toward regional crime analysis comes to the forefront of top issues in crime analysis, providing officers with information from outside agencies (federal, state, county, and other local law enforcement) that can assist officers and/or detectives in identifying crime series, trends, or possible suspects becomes increasingly important. Information on arrestees with specific MOs who may be responsible for incidents in the analyst's community should be spotlighted, again including a picture whenever possible. This information can be gathered from local, metro, regional, or statewide information sharing meetings.

Important note: You do not want to include information that could jeopardize another agency's ongoing investigations, so make sure they have cleared the information in your bulletin for publication.

Information from Investigations

Just as the dispatcher is curious as to how the call "came out," so too the officers in the field like to know if the suspect was ever charged or if the burglary was unfounded. In addition, when investigators are able to link crimes together with suspects, advising the officers of the status of a case or group of cases can benefit the investigation (as long as it is done properly).

For example: Detective Smith is investigating a group of juvenile auto burglars and suspects them of perpetrating fifteen recent apartment complex incidents where radar detectors were taken; however, he does not have enough evidence to bring up charges on the group. When this information is properly relayed to the street officers, they can take special note of the group and properly document any and all contacts with them. In fact, the patrol officers may even be able to use the information from investigations and the crime analysis unit to catch the perpetrators in the act.

Safety Tips

This is a legitimate "filler" for those times the analyst just wants the report to look pleasing to the reader. One- or two-line safety tips (often available from patrol sergeants, shift commanders, line officers, or the crime prevention unit) can be used to fill that last line or two in your bulletin to make it all look symmetrical. Be sure not to contradict any standard operating procedures.

For example: "Be sure to thoroughly check the back seat before *and* after transporting a prisoner in your patrol vehicle."

To Whom Should the Bulletins Be Distributed?

Think both internal and external.

Internal

- Officers (patrol, special units, and so on)
- Investigators
- Command staff
- Crime analysis unit
- Summer park/bike trail patrol
- Any others with a need-to-know status (This could include record clerks, dispatch, and so on, who are often able to "remind" officers of current trends or suspect information)

External

- Other local law enforcement (other local agencies, large and small)
- County law enforcement (sheriff's department, county jail, parole/probation, and so on)
- State law enforcement (state bureau of investigation, parole/probation, and so on)
- Federal law enforcement (FBI, IRS, ATF, Secret Service, postal inspectors, and so on)
- School security (elementary, secondary, college, and so on)
- Corrections officials
- Hospital security
- Housing officials

How Can They Be Distributed?

Internally

- Paper copies in mailboxes
- Roll calls/briefings
- E-mail
- Bulletin boards
- Reading files (three-ring binders located in each unit/chapter/division)

Externally

- Fax (Use a fax network and keep in mind that photos do not always fax well)
- E-mail (Watch security)
- Snail (postal) mail (Timeliness of data issues arise here)

Some Final Points About Creating Bulletins

- Consider having the same types of bulletins come out on the same days each week (arrest report on Mondays, crime sheet on Tuesdays, and so on).
- Get feedback from the officers and detectives as often as possible, both through informal and formal methods. Modify/discontinue the bulletins as appropriate. Remember—you are writing the bulletin for them, not yourself.
- Do not be afraid to change the bulletin (content or format). You do not have to wait for a new year to make changes.
- Even if you have a great, well-read bulletin, do not let it become stale or mundane.
- The ideal length for bulletins is one page—front and back (two pages in a Word/WordPerfect document sent through e-mail).
- Place bulletins in "reading files" and keep the reading files in locations handy for officers to read and review. These reading files should be separated allowing one chapter per type of bulletin and should contain year-to-date crime bulletins plus one year.
- Clearly label the agency name, bulletin name, and issue number at the top (so it is easy to refer back to them). Put the analyst's name and phone number on the top of the bulletin in plain view.

- Have your bulletins proofread by a secretary/administrative assistant prior to dissemination.
- Pick a font and use it consistently—do not change font type or size within the bulletin.
- Be sure the font you choose is also available on other department computers if disseminating through e-mail.
- If disseminating hard copies, select a colored paper specific only to your crime bulletins so that they are more easily recognized by staff as confidential documents (especially if found laying around the station in unsecured areas).
- Label sheets "Confidential" and "For police use only" when deemed appropriate to regulate dissemination.
- People love to see their names in print, especially if it is to praise an effort they have made. Recognize outstanding work by the patrol officers, investigators, or other sworn personnel in the bulletin. As mentioned earlier, this will help increase your readership.
- Remember that if you want the bulletin(s) to be taken seriously and to be considered a source of good intelligence information, you also must take them seriously. The idea is not to entertain the reader, but to inform the reader, providing timely, useful, and accurate information.

TYPES OF ADMINISTRATIVE CRIME ANALYSIS REPORTS

Some examples of automated (administrative) reports include, but are not limited to, the following:

Chief's Daily Report—contains information on the last twenty-four hours of crime in the city, broken down by crime type; month to date this year versus last year same month; year to date this year versus last year, year to date; and percentages related to the aforementioned information.

Chief's Weekly Report—similar to the chief's daily report; contains information on the last seven days of crime in the city.

Monthly Strategic Operations Plan—provides administration with information regarding not only Part I crime data (this month compared to last year, same month; this year, year-to-date compared to last year, same time, year-to-date) but also provides information on specific divisions, precincts, sectors, districts, shifts, and so on. May include information on response times, uses of force, citizen and internal complaints, traffic accident data, and other miscellaneous statistical information.

School Resource Officer or DARE Officer Report—generated daily, this report provides the name of any juvenile of school age involved in any type of incident or offense report made in the previous twenty-four hours. The information provided includes the student's name, age, school, and the location and report number for the incident.

Weekly Apartment Complex CAD (computer-aided dispatch) Report—A weekly report of all dispatched and self-initiated calls to each apartment complex participating in crime-free multihousing. These reports, which include the date, time, location, and type of incident, are provided to the apartment managers in an effort to keep management involved in holding tenants responsible for maintaining a safe, crime-free complex.

Field Interview Weekly Report—A complete report of the field interview forms or cards entered in the past week. Information included on this report includes the date, time, and location of contact and complete information regarding the subjects contacted and the reason for contact.

CAD (last twenty-four hour) Report—A complete report of all dispatched calls for the past twenty-four hours (in larger cities, this report may be divided into the calls for a particular precinct or division). Each dispatched call includes the complaint number (CAD generated), the location, unit(s) dispatched, times, the narrative comments entered by the dispatcher, and the disposition of the incident (e.g., report taken, handled by officer, canceled, and so on).

OTHER CRIME ANALYSIS PRODUCTS

In some law enforcement agencies, crime analysts are tasked with maintaining Web sites, conducting community surveys, and grant writing. If your agency is small, it may be that you are the only person available for these jobs. Although crime analysis involves research skills, it is best if the crime analyst is given the time and support needed to focus on analyzing crime rather than juggling a number of other roles. The quality of crime analysis suffers when the analyst has too many other responsibilities within an organization.

INTELLIGENCE ANALYSIS PRODUCTS

Some intelligence analysis products are listed and briefly defined below. This is by no means a comprehensive list, but intelligence analysts commonly produce the products mentioned.

- *Financial analysis:* Analysis of any relevant financial records and transactions, as well as the net worth of individuals suspected of criminal activities
- *Link analysis:* Charting of relationships among individuals, groups, and businesses involved in illegal enterprises
- *Telephone toll or record analysis:* Analysis of all data related to telephone calls for detection of members of criminal conspiracies through establishing the existence of telephone contacts between suspected individuals
- *Time lines:* A charting of activities based on time of occurrence—may be used in homicide investigations or other criminal investigations to display events over time

EVALUATION OF CRIME ANALYSIS PRODUCTS

All reports should be reviewed at least once a year to verify several things:

1. The information is still needed.
   a. Is the project the information was being used for complete?
   b. Is the requesting recipient still in the same position (job)?
      i. Is the new person using the information?
   c. Have there been any changes to the project?
      i. If so, the information output may need to be adjusted.
2. The recipient uses the information.
   a. Perhaps the focus of the project has changed and the information is no longer necessary.
   b. Maybe the recipient is receiving information from another source.

3. The information is accurate.
   a. Double-check the figures/information provided on the report to ensure no major glitches are preventing accurate information from being provided.
4. The information is useful.
   a. Does the intended audience have any suggestions that might make the product better?
   b. Would changing the format of the product assist the customer in any way?
   c. Is unnecessary information provided?
   d. Is the report lacking information that should be provided?
5. The information is timely.
   a. Is the customer receiving the product in a timely manner?
   b. Would it be possible to have the report automated and printed on the customer's computer?
   c. Would other arrangements for receiving the information be more practical?
      i. Customer picks up the information.
      ii. The information is sent via the intranet rather than interdepartmental mail or snail mail.

There are three different classes of products with regards to frequency: daily, weekly/monthly, and by request only. Obviously, the more frequently the product is produced, whether automatically or manually created by an analyst, the less frequent feedback and evaluation are needed. In other words, if you are producing an automatic, daily chief's report (administrative crime analysis), there is no need to ask for feedback on the product each day. Rather, semiannually or perhaps annually, contact the recipients of the reports to review the timeliness, usefulness, accuracy, and ongoing need for the product. At that time, changes and modifications can be made to the report to ensure that the crime analysis unit produces ongoing quality products for the intended customers.

When dealing with weekly/monthly reports, an analyst should contact some or all of the recipients three to four times a year to ensure the report/product continues to be useful and contains all of the necessary information. Weekly crime bulletins (tactical or strategic) should be reviewed by some or all of the recipients as part of an ongoing process to continue to evolve the report into the most presentable, most useful, and most timely product possible. As feedback is received from the intended audience, the analyst can make changes to the document immediately. Not only do the changes show the audience that the analyst is listening and adapting, but it also helps keep the audience involved in what is essentially *their* report (*not* the analyst's report).

By-request-only reports are much more cut and dried. Any time a new product, that is, something different from previous products produced, is provided to a targeted audience, the analyst should request feedback on its usefulness. The analyst should not only look at whether or not the information provided was useful but also what other types of information could have been included that might have made the report better. When providing a "by request" product, the analyst may want to attach a simple questionnaire/feedback form with some or all of the following questions:

- Was the information useful?
- Is the product you received more/less than expected?
- What changes would you have made to the product?
- How can this type of information be better presented in the future?

Do not spend time making products no one values. Do not indulge in research that your department cannot utilize. Be creative—do not get stuck in fitting the information you have into tried-and-true formats—use the tools you have to fit the problem. Create bulletins and reports specific to problems *after* you decide what it is you want to communicate.

RESOURCES FOR CRIME ANALYSIS PRODUCTS

Crime Analysis and Mapping Product Templates are available online to assist you in developing your own crime analysis products. Mary Velasco, Jim Griffin, and Rachel Boba of the Police Foundation produced the templates for the USDOJ's Office of Community Oriented Policing. The Web site address for the templates is <http://www.policefoundation.org/docs/mapping-templates.html>. The following templates are available:

- Annual report
- Map layout

- Memo
- Persons bulletin
- Regular report
- Tactical bulletin
- Web page table of contents

The appendix of this book offers you some examples of crime analysis products. Contact other crime analysis units and request samples of their products for more ideas.

Chapter 6

Advice for the New Crime Analyst

A new crime analyst faces a challenging road; often there are few peers present, and little guidance from within the hiring law enforcement organization. This chapter will offer advice and perspectives from working crime analysts to help the new analyst get a head start in his or her new profession. The following passage introduces the new analyst to what it is like to work in the field.

"A DAY IN THE LIFE OF A CRIME ANALYST"

0722. Arrive at work. Before I can reach my office, a lieutenant who asks if I can join a committee on evaluating the efficiency of using sworn or civilian staff to perform crime scene processing functions stops me. I mention to the lieutenant that this issue has been studied ad nauseum, and that management has never reached a decision on this. The lieutenant says that he is using this issue for his master's thesis and thinks management is in a better position to listen. Ah ha!

0734. Rev up computer and check voice mail. How can I have three messages when I left after 5:00 last night? Make notes and check calendar for schedule. Check e-mail (I can't believe this post—who else can I forward it to??)

0800. Get coffee and stop by boss's office to see what's up for the day. He passes along a request from the chief and asks if I

"A Day in the Life of a Crime Analyst," by Cheri Cohn, formerly of Lakewood Police Department, from the Colorado Crime Analysis Association newsletter, p. 3, Second Quarter, 1999. Printed with permission from Cheri Cohn.

can provide a call for service map next week for presentation to city council. Since I don't have a plotter, this means extra work to have it printed in another building. I wonder if this is the time to remind him that I don't have a plotter but decide to let it pass for now. Of course I can get this to the chief, I tell my boss. Also reminded him that I would like his feedback on the last report I left on his desk. On the way back to my office, a detective who wants to know—right now—how to retrieve information on a death investigation.

0819. Query the information on a death investigation and make a note to the detective how she can retrieve it, too. Begin returning voice mail. A manager from an apartment complex calls regarding some information she received on crime in her area. She wants to know why there are so many car break-ins. She is new to her job, and we discuss efforts police have made to work with both residents and previous managers on crime prevention. I pass her concerns along to crime prevention and the watch commander. Return call from coordinator for city training committee to set up meeting. Begin reviewing last night's log and case reports.

1000. Meet with programmer to clarify information on CAD data fields. (It's not as though anyone ever documented this information before; can it be that no one has ever needed to retrieve it before? It's no wonder officers question why we have to collect so much data.) After discussion, I realize that one field I have used in queries was probably in error, and wonder how many times I may have pulled wrong information. Also discuss status of Records' data submission to CBI and launch into lengthy discussion on what is wrong with system. Stop in administration to pick up my mail, drop off a medical reimbursement form in employee relations, get another cup of coffee, and return to my office.

1110. A detective stops by my office with a stack of case reports and asks if I can help him with this investigation. Thinking that it's something really exciting, I reply enthusiastically that I'd be glad to. He asks me to review reports (there are over sixty) for any commonalities. I realize the detective doesn't want to do his own work and read the reports and is pawning it off on me, and tell him it would be a few days before I can get back to him.

1142. Check phone mails; lunch plans canceled. I think I have a Lean Cuisine in freezer. Microwave is in use—I'll check later. In response to request from the city manager's office, I retrieve my most recent crime trends report and begin writing a summary for an article on crime trends.

1222. Microwave is still in use. Chat with an investigator on his progress with burglary investigation. He asks if I can get him information on any known suspects with similar MOs to his pattern. Finally get my Lean Cuisine in microwave.

1243. Continue writing summary for city manager's office, aware that I have to be careful to not mention anything that may get citizens too upset, and forward it to my supervisor for chief's approval before it gets published.

1413. Query burglary pattern and read reports that fit pattern. Since burglaries appear to be by someone on foot, query suspect information for known suspects living within two miles of location of burglary pattern and potential suspect residences.

1631. Query information in response to media request on whether there are more sex assaults on children in the summer months and forward to public information officer.

1714. Rush off to pick up my son from baseball practice and promise him that I will never, never be late again.

TIPS FOR THE NEW CRIME ANALYST

- Prioritizing work and managing time efficiently and effectively are important. As illustrated by Cheri Cohn, a crime analyst usually has a number of requests to work on simultaneously. Develop good time-management skills; be organized.

- Although you may have a staggering workload, find at least one area to excel in, whether it is forecasting, spatial analysis, or a specific crime specialty, where you routinely conduct thorough analysis and uncover series.
- Do not promise work you cannot deliver. Doing so will make it difficult for you to achieve credibility in your organization.
- Be aware that you have bias, both conscious and unconscious, and make every attempt to be objective and realistic in your work. Presumptuousness, overconfidence, oversimplification, conservatism, ignorance—these mind-sets can be pitfalls in analytical work. Do not assume that all people think the way you do or see things in the same fashion (Krizan 1999).
- Log your work. Track it in a systematic way. This will help you justify requests for more staff or clerical help and will also help you keep track of all requests for service.
- Identify your work. Put your name and title on everything you produce, including maps.
- Learn how to develop your own simple databases for specific crimes. Customized databases will permit you to choose your own information fields and collect information in a mode that makes analysis easier for you.
- If you work in a crime analysis unit, maximize effectiveness by optimal use of the strengths of individual unit staff. If someone loves GIS and another person excels at administrative analysis, divide tasks so that each person does what he or she does best. However, all staff should be cross-trained and be able to cover for one another.
- Do not reinvent the wheel—when you are stuck ask other crime analysts for advice. Many contacts are listed in this book, and if you attend conferences or association meetings, you will meet others. Do not be afraid to ask for help. If your agency has affiliations with local colleges or universities, you may be able to enlist their expert help for free.
- Share your knowledge. This field needs a set of "best practices," a body of knowledge regarding what works. It is up to all of us to share what we know to help crime analysis grow as a profession.

- Maintain high ethical standards. Crime analysis is, at its core, about searching for truth. Integrity is crucial.
- Continually learn.
- People skills *are* important. Listen carefully and do not be afraid to ask questions if requests for crime analysis services are not clearly articulated. Develop good relationships within your department and in your region.
- Keep confidential information in locked cabinets. Be conscientious about security and privacy rules. In any "gray" areas, err on the side of caution.
- Remember that data quality is the key to success. Strive to improve the quality of data gathering in your organization.

Understand Obstacles to Crime Analysis Success

New crime analysts should also be aware of some of the reasons crime analysis is currently misunderstood and underappreciated in police departments. Awareness of these issues will help you understand resistance and lack of support for your role in your agency.

- Crime analysis goes against the traditional reactive approach to policing. Implementing major change is difficult in established organizations.
- Crime analysis is more reflective than action oriented. Police have been conditioned by the demand to respond to emergency calls to take action rather than study or reflect about the nature of problems.
- Crime analysis often points out more problems than solutions.
- The role of crime analysis and the crime analyst within the police departments are not well defined or understood, even in agencies that have had crime analysts for years.
- Policymakers do not envision the potentials of crime analysis as a systematic process within law enforcement. This is because crime analysis as a specific function is new and not well understood both within and outside of law enforcement.
- The lack of quality information in many police departments struggling with information technology problems interferes with the ability of analysts and officers to effectively analyze crime.

Understanding these issues will help you as you work toward meeting the challenges of analyzing crime in your agency.

Join Valuable Listservs

Currently there are two main listservs that are the most helpful for crime analysts. On these computer mailing lists you may post questions and read the questions and answers of others working in the field. Some persons complain that there is too much e-mail to read when one belongs to such lists, but listservs do help crime analysts stay connected to the people and learn about new topics in the field. If you are the only crime analyst in your agency, the listservs allow you to be part of a global community of analysts, thus you are never truly "alone." Joining is highly recommended.

To join "LEAnalyst"—a listserv that connects over 1,000 persons in the field of law enforcement analysis, go to the Web site: <http://www.inteltec.com>.

For information and instructions on how to join the "Crimemap" listserv, sponsored by the National Institute of Justice's Crime Mapping Research Center, go to the Web site: <http://www.ojp.usdoj.gov/cmrc/faq/listserv_faq.html>.

The FBI has a dial-up information-sharing site called "LEO Online." This is a restricted site; the chief officer of your law enforcement agency must sign any applications. Confidential and/or restricted information can be exchanged securely via the LEO site, so if you have classified information to share, this is a good method to protect privacy yet connect with other law enforcers who may be able to help your situation. Thus, it can be worthwhile to join. Crime analysts can benefit from this type of information sharing; this service also provides online tutorials for improving computer skills. For a LEO application contact:

> LEO Program Office
> FBI Headquarters
> Room 11259
> 935 Pennsylvania Avenue, NW
> Washington, DC 20535
> 202-324-8833
> <http://www.tahn.org/LEOapplication.pdf>

Join a Professional Association

In the early 1990s the International Association of Crime Analysts (IACA) was formed and became recognized as the professional association for crime analysts. The IACA was formed to provide assistance to agencies starting crime analysis units and to make crime analysis training available. According to the current IACA Web site:

> The International Association of Crime Analysts hereby organizes to enhance effectiveness and consistency in the fields of crime and intelligence analysis. To this end, the IACA is dedicated to advocacy for professional standards, to providing practical educational opportunities, and to the creation of an international network for the standardization of analytic techniques. (http://www.iaca.net/about/bylaws.html)

The International Association of Law Enforcement Intelligence Analysts (IALEIA) is another professional organization created to support law enforcement analysts. It is recommended that an analyst join one or both of these associations for several important reasons.

- *Peer support:* An analyst working alone receives invaluable support by attending conferences and meeting other analysts through these organizations. Analysts who work with analysts in a unit also benefit from this support—the fact is, there are not many law enforcement analysts in most cities, and networking helps ease the sense of professional isolation.
- *Education and training:* The associations provide education and training through publications, conferences, and their Web sites.
- *Certification:* The IACA is currently developing a certification process that will help professionalize crime analysis. IALEIA has developed a certification program. Information on certification is provided at the end of this chapter.
- *Information:* Current information on employment opportunities, training, and crime/intelligence analysis is available through the associations.

Regional crime and intelligence analysis associations can be found in some parts of the country. These organizations provide all the benefits of the international organizations, but also provide the opportunity to share information relevant to ongoing crime series, patterns, and trends in a certain area. Networking at this level can help an analyst more effectively work for his or her agency.

Sergeant Dan Barber has provided a great example of the advantages of this type of communication:

> I am a supervisor in a ten-person detective bureau. My department, Boulder County Sheriff's Department, in Boulder, Colorado, has a sworn population of about 175 deputies working at the jail and about fifty deputies working in patrol and as detectives. The population of Boulder County is approximately 250,000, with 180,000 within the sheriff's jurisdiction. Our county is 750 square miles with approximately 400 square miles of mountains. We do not currently have a crime analysis unit. We do have crime summaries completed twice a month by reserve officers or volunteer workers.
>
> Even though I do not have the intense crime generated by a densely populated area, we recognize that criminals are transient and cross all jurisdictions. My department has joined the Colorado Crime Analysis Association. This is a group of crime analysts who meet regularly and share crime information on what is occurring in their jurisdictions. I have found that attending these monthly meetings has been helpful in working together to successfully identify and apprehend criminals.
>
> A case in point: After attending one meeting in the spring of 1999, I received a call from a Longmont PD crime analyst in reference to a rash of burglaries. We compared notes referencing several burglaries that had occurred at veterinary clinics within our own jurisdictions. County patrol officers had done a field interview on likely suspects driving a yellow Camaro that was similar to one that was seen in the area of one burglary. Both departments worked together and initiated surveillance on the possible suspects. During one surveillance, we followed the suspects to a vet clinic and they were scared off before making an entry. Search warrants were executed and stolen drugs were recovered. Three suspects were soon arrested and charged in the burglaries. This investigation cleared eight burglaries that had occurred in three counties and four cities.

Departments that do not have crime analysts can benefit from the departments around them that do.

Associations for Crime Analysts on the Web

- International Association of Crime Analysts
  <http://www.iaca.net/>

- International Association of Law Enforcement Intelligence Analysts
  <http://www.ialeia.org/>
- Mid-America Regional Crime Analysis Network (MARCAN)
  <www.marcan.org>
- Arizona Association of Crime Analysts
  <http://aaofca.tripod.com/>
- Southern California Crime and Intelligence Analyst Association
- Inland Empire Crime Analysis & Intelligence Association (California)
  <www.crimeanalyst.org>
  Florida Crime and Intelligence Analysts Association
  <www.FCIAA.org>
- Massachusetts Association of Crime Analysts
  <http://www.macrimeanalysts.com>
- Texas Crime and Intelligence Analysts
  <http://www.tacia.org>

Other Crime Analysis Association Contact Information

Northern Valley Crime and Intelligence Analyst Association (NoVCIAA)
Rick Blankenship
<viceprez@crimeanalyst.org>

Bay Area Crime and Intelligence Analysts Association (BACIAA) (California)
Karen Vincent
510-293-7068
<adminmember2@crimeanalyst.org>

Ohio Association of Crime Analysts (OACA)
Bill Ulvila
216-623-5576
<ulvilaw@aol.com>

Massachusetts Association of Crime Analysts (MACA)
Christopher Bruce

978-774-1212 ext. 119
<cbruce@mail.danvers-ma.org>

Inland Empire Crime Analysis & Intelligence Association (IECIAA)
Rhonda Maher
909-387-0334
<treasurer@crimeanalyst.org>

Texas Association of Crime & Intelligence Analysts (TACIA)
David Jimenez
915-834-8628
<david.jimenez@usdoj.gov>

Northwest Regional Crime Analysis Network (NORCAN)
Kim Hathaway
509-585-4336
<kim-hathaway@ci.kennewick.wa.us>

Arizona Association of Crime Analysts (AACA)
Connie Kostelac
602-262-7163
<ckostela@ci.phoenix.az.us>

Florida Association of Crime and Intelligence Analysts (FCIAA)
Metre Lewis
407-847-0176 ext. 3256
<mlewis@kissimmee.org>

Western New York Regional Association of Crime and Intelligence Analysts (WNYRACIA)
Deborah Osborne
716-851-5058
<daosborne@bpd.ci.buffalo.ny.us>

Utah Law Enforcement Analyst Association
Peggy Call
801-799-3878
<peggy.call@ci.slc.ut.us>

Mid-America Regional Crime Analysis Network
Tim Layman

816-235-1555
<laymant@umkc.edu>

Colorado Crime Analyst Network
Lori Frank
970-416-2515
<lfrank@fcgov.com>

Southern California Crime and Intelligence Association
Carol Wiseman
661-267-4321
<president@scciaa.org>

San Diego Crime and Intelligence Analyst Association
Latonya Gridiron
760-432-4936
<Lgridiron@ci.escondido.ca.us>

International Association of Crime Analysts
Noah Fritz
1-800-416-8086
<www.iaca.net>
<nfritz@du.edu>

Explore Certification Options

The Society of Certified Criminal Analysts

The Society of Certified Criminal Analysts was established by the International Association of Law Enforcement Intelligence Analysts in 1989. It offers two levels of certification—regular and lifetime. Applicants must be members of IALEIA or AIPIO (Australian Institute of Professional Intelligence Officers). In addition, completion of basic analytical training and sponsorship by a member of the SCCA Board of Governors is required.

Regular certification criteria include completion of two years of college or five years of professional experience in a law enforcement agency, currently working as an analyst (sworn or nonsworn), and passing the written test and practex. Lifetime certification criteria include completion of four years of college and having ten years of analytical experience. Exemplary performance in one area may balance the necessary criteria for consideration by the SCCA Board of Governors. For more information visit: <http://www.ialeia.org/scca/>

The International Association of Crime Analysts

The International Association of Crime Analysts is in the process of developing a certification program for analysts, with an anticipated first test to be offered in 2004. Tentatively, to qualify to take the certification exam, individuals will have to have three years of working experience as a law enforcement or intelligence analyst and attain a qualifying number of points on a point system. The point system is based on various types of education and experience. Training for skill set development will be offered at IACA conferences, but it will not be mandatory for certification; individuals may receive education training elsewhere.

The skill sets identified for certification and their definitions, as posted on the Web site (www.iaca.net, January 2003) are as follows.

Knowledge of crime analysis basics. Have an understanding and knowledge of the definition of crime analysis, as well as the types, functions, and processes of crime analysts and crime analysis.

Evaluate the integrity of information. Have the ability to determine the validity, reliability, and credibility of verbal, written, numeric, and graphic information encountered during the analysis process.

Knowledge of criminal behavior. Understand the behavioral patterns (Method of Operation) and motivations of serial criminals, street criminals, organized crime groups, juveniles, domestic/family violence, and the impact of alcohol and narcotics on crime.

Understand socioeconomic, cultural, psychological, biological, environmental, and historical theories/influences on criminal behavior. Have knowledge of victimology.

Understand criminal justice system. Understand the relationship among law enforcement, courts, and corrections at the local, state, and federal level. Have knowledge of how people and cases progress through the system, of the professions and roles within the system, and of the function of crime analysis within this context.

Conduct temporal analysis. Know how to calculate and analyze the times of day, days of week, intervals, durations, tempos, and temporal cycles of crime in general and of criminal behavior in short-term and long-term series, patterns, and trends. Understand the use of temporal analysis in making forecasts and predictions of future incidents regarding identified crime trends and series.

Use descriptive statistics. Know how to summarize and analyze qualitative and quantative data using calculations such as frequencies, percent change, cross-tabulations, measures of central tendency (e.g., mean, median, mode), measures of variation (e.g., standard deviation, variance), and correlations. Understand the difference between, and appropriate usage of, ordinal, nominal, interval, and ratio data. Know the appropriate levels of measurement used to support tactical, strategic, and administrative analysis.

Use inferential statistics. Know the difference between inferential and descriptive statistics and when each is appropriate to crime analysis. Know the techniques for taking random samples and how the results of these samples can be inferentially applied to the populations from which they were drawn. Examples include taking a random sample of citizens to survey for problem-solving purposes or victimization studies within one's jurisdiction or taking a random sample of crimes or calls-for-service.

Conduct demographic analysis. Have the ability to gather from various sources, analyze and summarize demographic information such as population, housing data, racial/ethnic makeup, and age groups, and to understand the relationship and application possibilities of these variables to crime data in the context of community policing and problem solving.

Interpret crime statistics. Have the ability to understand and compare local and national crime statistics (e.g., Uniform Crime Report [UCR] and National Incident Based Reporting System [NIBRS] data*) using common data standards, codebooks, and data dictionaries. Understand the rules and standards, as well as the caveats and shortcomings, of these data sets.

Spatial analysis. Know the basic principles of geographic analysis, and how to create maps by using appropriate data sets. Know how to produce point symbol (pin) maps, buffer maps, hot spot, and density maps. Be able to analyze maps to determine the nature of crime problems related to location, to use maps in forecasting and predicting future incidents of crime trends and series, and to interpret maps

---

*Analysts from outside the United States will apply the standard to their national statistics.

for specific audiences. Have knowledge of issues integral to crime mapping (e.g., geocoding, privacy, data quality).

Investigative/intelligence analysis charting. Create visual work products, such as link analysis and visual investigative analysis charts, which depict information that can further investigations and intelligence efforts.

Reading comprehension. Have the ability to discern, synthesize, remember, and summarize useful and logical information from a report, research document, or other written information source.

Writing expository narratives. Possess the necessary writing skills to explain information, draw conclusions, and/or make recommendations in a narrative format that is objective, succinct, pertinent, articulate, and relevant. .

Making effective presentations. The ability to develop an effective, directed, and informative verbal presentation that will be useful to the specific audience being addressed; the knowledge of visual aide software and operation; the ability to handle audience participation and time constraints and to answer questions concisely and accurately.

Word processing skills. Know how to use a computer to produce documents such as bulletins and reports, which are suitable for dissemination to various audiences, and to incorporate graphics into these documents (i.e., charts, maps, pictures, diagrams).

Spreadsheet operations. Use a computer to create an electronic matrix or spreadsheet, manipulate the data and/or records and use statistical formulae to answer fundamental questions including frequency, percent, percent change, sum, average, standard deviation, regression analysis, forecasting, and correlation. Know how to perform cross-tabulations, to create charts and graphs, and to export these objects to other applications.

Internet/intranet skills. Know how the Internet/intranet can be accessed, how to use internal and Web-based e-mail, and how to use search engines. Know about online resources and crime analysis-related information that can be found on the Internet and on various intranets. Have the ability to find and use relevant and "open source" information.

Applied research methods in crime analysis. Know how to conduct applied research, through familiarity with basic research methodologies. Understand the scientific process of collection, collation, analysis, and evaluation, and how crime analysis represents social science as applied research. Have an understanding of the concepts and the usage of the SARA problem-solving process (Scan, Analyze, Response, and Assess).

Evaluation of qualitative information. Have the ability to analyze the content of qualitative information such as survey results, crime and arrest reports, narratives, and victim/witness/suspect statements. Have the ability to understand, categorize, and summarize qualitative data, and to include relevant qualitative information in reports and briefings.

Critical thinking skills. Have knowledge of the importance of thinking critically about the methods, procedures, tools, and techniques employed in crime analysis. Know how the following elements of critical thinking apply to law enforcement analytical work: inductive and deductive reasoning, logic, problem-solving techniques, creativity, self-awareness, and self-regulation.

The development of professional certification criteria for crime analysts is a major step toward making crime analysis a true profession. Some analysts take the courses offered through the Alpha Group (see Chapter 8) to acquire certification in crime and intelligence analysis through the state of California. Chapter 8 lists some other programs that offer credentials in crime and/or intelligence analysis.

The following "Ten Commandments of Crime Analysis" is a practical and entertaining outlook on the role of the crime analyst in local law enforcement.* It offers great advice and direction for those new to the field, as well as to veterans of crime analysis.

"THE TEN COMMANDMENTS OF CRIME ANALYSIS"

1. Thy Task Is Crime Analysis. Thou Shalt Have No Other Tasks Before It.

Crime analysts tend to become technological wizards in a relatively short time, given the number of computer applications vital to modern crime analysis. This computer proficiency tends to make a mark on the other members of your department, and eventually you find yourself mired in requests to develop a database for the Internal Affairs Unit, to crunch citation

---

"The Ten Commandments of Crime Analysis" is printed with permission from Christopher W. Bruce, Crime Analyst, Danvers (MA) Police Department.

numbers for the Traffic Unit, and to help an investigator design a flyer for his upcoming housewarming party!

On the other hand, maybe your unit has simply developed an overall "reputation for competency," so that when anything important needs doing, the command staff tends to "give it to crime analysis." Whatever the case, you must develop techniques to put your primary task—crime analysis—at the top of your list every day.

2. Thou Shalt Read Thy Department's Crime Reports Every Day.

Too many crime analysts try to find trends and crime patterns by looking up the information in their records management system (RMS) or computer-aided dispatch (CAD) system. This approach presents many problems with timeliness, accuracy, and information sufficiency. You want your information to be accurate and timely. Furthermore, you want to have access to the full text of every crime report so you can correctly identify modus operandi and categorization. To this end, you will find no substitute for reading, every day, copies of all crime and arrest reports taken by your department.

3. Thou Shalt Track and Control Thine Own Information.

Another problem with records management systems: they generally do not have fields that allow you to enter information vital to crime analysis. Such information may include point of entry (for burglaries), type of premises, categorization or classification, whether you have identified the crime as part of a pattern or series, and many other modus operandi factors.

If you want to track this information across a period of time—and trust us, you do—you will probably find your RMS inadequate. You should develop your own means for recording crime patterns, and crime conducive to patterns, in your jurisdiction. Methods for this include matrices, spreadsheets, and—probably most ideal—customized databases.

4. Honor Thine Patrol Officers and Investigators.

Remember, the job of a crime analyst involves identifying crime patterns and trends so that the patrol and investigative divisions can develop strategies and allocate resources. You are a tool for their use, not the other way around. If you become aloof from or hostile to your patrol and investigative divisions, you will probably fail as a crime analysis unit.

Crime analysis is impossible without accurate information, and patrol officers and investigators are fonts of information. Unfortunately, much of this information is undocumented. You may have identified and analyzed a pattern of robberies in the South Central District, but only Sergeant Jones knows that he saw a pack of suspicious-looking kids hanging out there the night before last. You will need to develop a good rapport with your officers and investigators in order to facilitate the exchange of this type of information.

5. Thou Shalt Never Present Statistics (or Maps) Alone.

"There are lies, damned lies, and statistics" is a quote variously attributed to Samuel Clemens, Winston Churchill, Benjamin Disraeli, Karl Marx, and Theodore Roosevelt. In many cases, this is true. Statistics presented alone, with no comparison or context, are like nuclear power: they can be used for good or evil.

Never present statistics by themselves. Statistics are indicators; your job as a crime analyst is to interpret them. Never say "There were thirty housebreaks in the Old Port neighborhood last month" and leave it at that. Statistics must be comparative, descriptive, and accompanied by qualitative analysis: "There were thirty housebreaks in the Old Port neighborhood last month. This is up twenty percent from the previous month and thirty-five percent from the same period last year. The average neighborhood in the city averages fifteen housebreaks per month. Of the thirty housebreaks last month, ten were crude, kick-in-the-door-and-steal-the-VCR jobs (which is usual), but twenty were sophisticated breaks in which alarm systems were circumvented and expensive oil paintings and oriental rugs were stolen. This is an unusual modus operandi for the city, and we therefore attribute the increase in burglaries to a new professional burglary ring that is at work in the city."

6. Thou Shalt Know Thy Jurisdiction from One End unto the Other.

The first task of any new crime analyst should be to get to know his or her city or town. If you are an officer-analyst with several years of patrol under your belt, this probably won't be a problem for you. Civilian analysts, however, may know little or nothing about the city when they start their jobs. This can result in some comical blunders. You don't want to report a "major pattern" of shoplifting at 100 Main Street if 100 Main Street is a megaplex mall where shoplifting occurs every day.

Very quickly, you will want to learn the street layouts, the major parks and public areas, the major commercial areas, the neighborhood boundaries, the ethnic enclaves, the economic situation of each area of the city, the locations of public housing projects, and generally where people live, where they work, and where they spend their free time in your jurisdiction.

As you grow as a crime analyst, however, you will want to know more. Your ability to analyze patterns and to recommend strategies will be much greater if you have personally visited the crime "hot spots," patronized the commercial areas, and driven through the depressed residential areas.

7. Thou Shalt Not Stop Crime Analysis at Thy Jurisdiction's Borders.

There's an old legend about King Arthur. One day, Merlin turned him into a goose and let him fly across England. As Arthur sailed through the air, he surveyed the landscape below him. He saw mountains, and rivers, and plains, and cities, but he realized to his astonishment that he couldn't tell where one country began and the other one ended. There were no lines on the ground—as there were on maps—to mark the political geography that men held so dear.

Work with maps long enough [and] you'll start to unconsciously think of the areas outside your jurisdiction's borders as blank white tundra. These imaginary lines need to be unimagined for at least two reasons. First, while your police administrators may value the difference between one side of a border and another, you can be sure that your criminals do not care. If you have a crime series that potentially crosses another jurisdiction's boundaries, you'll want to get together with your counterpart over there to see if they're experiencing it too. You can both help each other out with information. Many departments are experimenting with regional information-sharing systems—but until a regional "system" comes to your jurisdiction, a few simple telephone calls once or twice a week can have impressive results.

8. Who, What, When, Where, How, and Why Are Thy Children. Thou Shalt Not Favor One Over the Others.

Proper analysis of crime patterns and trends involves careful consideration of all factors. New technologies tend to give emphasis to certain factors over others—the advent of "crime mapping," in particular, tends to overemphasize the "where" factor. Departments with advanced GIS systems often rely on their mapping to identify all crime patterns, even though many patterns do not show themselves in neat clusters—finding these patterns usually involves a careful reading of the modus operandi, or the "how" factor (see Commandment 2).

The key to crime analysis, like all things in life, is balance. Both effective identification and effective description of a crime pattern requires the intelligent consideration of factors like victim and suspect characteristics (who), the type of crime (what), the time, day, and date (when), the modus operandi (how), the cause or offender motivation (why), and of course the location, type of premises, and geography (where). Make sure all factors are considered in your analysis.

9. Remember Thy Community and Keep It Holy.

In the end, your boss is not your direct supervisor, nor is it your bureau head, nor is it your commissioner or chief. You ultimately work for the people who live, work, and play in your jurisdiction, and your job, like the job of the police department as a whole, is to make their lives safer. Anything that accomplishes this goal (e.g., daily tactical crime analysis) should be your A1 priority. Anything that is not related to this goal (e.g., administrative reports) should take a lower priority. Anything that is antithetical to this goal (e.g., blowing off pattern analysis for a week, caving in to departmental encouragement to "hedge" the numbers) should not be done at all.

Try to remember that there are dozens—or perhaps hundreds or thousands—of people who have not been victimized because of your work. If you identify and thus help your department stop a pattern after four incidents instead of a dozen, that's eight people who weren't burglarized, robbed, or vandalized because of you. They'll never know it, and you'll never know them, but never forget that they exist.

10. Thou Shalt Not Covet Thy Neighbor's Neural Network.

If you're a new crime analysis unit, sooner or later you're going to attend a regional or national conference on crime analysis, where you'll discover that the police department up the street is using neural networks, is engaged in data mining, and is conducting raster mapping. You'll realize with shock that you don't even know what these terms *mean*.

Stop the feelings of inadequacy and inferiority before they start and remember this: 75 percent of the benefit of crime analysis is achieved through the basic tasks of reading reports, looking for crime problems, and issuing bulletins to your department.

Neural networks and other advanced technologies are helpful for certain departments, but then, we've met crime analysts who talk about neural networks but who couldn't identify a serial rapist if he was spelling his name across the city, and we've met brilliant crime analysts who couldn't find the power switch on a computer. Advanced technologies, like basic skills, are only tools with which you perform your essential duty identifying, analyzing, and reporting crime patterns and trends. Your superiority as a crime analyst will depend on how well you do your job, not on what tools you use to do it.

Good luck to the new crime analyst!

Chapter 7

Creating a Crime Analysis Unit

This chapter addresses several considerations involved in creating a crime analysis unit, including policies and procedures, defining the role of the crime analysis unit within the department, marketing and funding, and resources for crime analysis.

POLICIES AND PROCEDURES FOR CRIME ANALYSIS

Developing policies and procedures for crime analysis is a part of implementing crime analysis in a local law enforcement agency. Not all agencies have formalized policies and procedures in effect; nevertheless, defining agency policy and procedures can be helpful in delineating the role of crime analysis in an organization.

A Mission Statement

A mission statement is a simple way to begin setting crime analysis policy. It can help focus the direction of a crime analysis unit, even if the "unit" itself is simply a one-person operation. Here is an example of a crime analysis mission statement written by crime analyst Michelle Arneson, Green Bay, Wisconsin:

> The Green Bay Police Department's Crime Analysis Unit strives to serve as the "information hub" of the department by gathering, analyzing, utilizing, and disseminating information that is relevant and useful in supporting other units of the department to prevent, deter, solve, and prosecute criminal activity.

Policy and Procedures

Because of state and local accreditation criteria, many agencies are developing policies that call for analysis of crime. The Commission on Accreditation for Law Enforcement Agencies, Inc. (CALEA) publishes a guide, *Standards for Law Enforcement Agencies: The Standards Manual of the Law Enforcement Agency Accreditation Program* (1994). Information on standards for crime analysis as policy for law enforcement is outlined. To order a copy of this book contact:

> Commission on Accreditation for Law Enforcement Agencies, Inc.
> 10306 Eaton Place, Suite 32
> Fairfax, Virginia 22030-2201
> 703-352-4225
> 703-591-2206 Fax

The International Association of Chiefs of Police (IACP) offers model policy and procedures for crime analysis. For information on ordering the Crime Analysis Model Policy, contact the IACP at 1-800-THE-IACP.

Formulating standard operating procedures for the crime analysis unit helps define its role within the organization. Standard operating procedures may contain the following elements:

- The purpose of the crime analysis unit and the documented procedures
- To whom the procedures apply
- The methods used by crime analysis
- The data used by crime analysis
- The products to be produced by crime analysis
- The dissemination of reports generated by crime analysis, including any restrictions
- Methods of assessing the crime analysis information and the functioning of the crime analysis unit
- Performance evaluations

CONSIDERATIONS IN CREATING A CRIME ANALYSIS UNIT

As a law enforcement agency expands in crime analysis function, the following questions are often considered:

- Do you use sworn officers or hire civilians?
- Do you use volunteers or interns to supplement staff?
- Where should the unit be located?
- Should it be centralized or decentralized?
- How do we promote staff interactions?

The authors surveyed a number of crime analysis units and compiled answers for some of these questions in Table 7.1.

Staffing

When the decision to create a crime analysis unit is made, it has often stemmed from one of two reasons: (1) in order to become accredited, the agency must incorporate crime analysis, or (2) the chief and/or command staff has a particular interest in using crime analysis to complement the community-oriented policing and problem-solving philosophy. Basically, either crime analysis is "forced" upon an agency or "requested" in an agency. Despite the fact that both result in the creation of a unit (whether the unit consists of a half-time person, a full-time person, or a full staff), the support that the unit receives may be directly related to whether the unit was forced or requested.

One of the first issues that a commander will have to deal with is staffing the crime analysis unit. Whether the position(s) should be filled with sworn or nonsworn personnel is an issue to consider carefully. Oftentimes, police personnel look to experienced officers and/or detectives, knowing that their natural base of knowledge and intuition regarding criminal activity is very relevant to the position of crime analyst. Additionally, as these sworn officers are familiar with the jurisdiction, the known offenders, and the workings of the department, and since they are already employees, transferring them to the new unit seems appropriate and logical. In many departments, sworn personnel fully staff crime analysis units; however, the undeniable trend is toward civilian personnel.

Civilians often are able to bring qualities to the unit that sworn personnel may not possess. These include computer skills, backgrounds in qualitative and quantitative analysis, research skills, writing skills, and mathematical skills. Civilians are also more likely to stay in this

TABLE 7.1. Crime Analysis Unit Survey Responses

Agency	Year Crime Analysis Began	Titles	Number of Staff	Sworn or Civilian	Interns or Volunteers
Akron Police Department, Ohio	May 1998	Law Enforcement Planners	3	civilian	graduate interns
Austin Police Department, Texas	1998 (real "unit" formed)	Crime Analyst Associate Crime Analyst Crime Analyst Senior	9 and 1 supervisor	civilian	both
Boulder Police Department, Colorado	1975	Crime Analyst Technical Research Analyst	2 + ½-time administrative clerk	civilian	both
Buffalo Police Department, New York	1997	Crime Analyst	1	civilian	interns
Cambridge Police Department, Massachusetts	1979	Senior Crime Analyst Crime Analyst	2 + clerical support	civilian	interns

Department		Position			
Charlotte-Mecklenburg Police Department, North Carolina	late 1970s	GIS Management Analysts GIS Coordinator GIS Applications Specialist Crime Analyst	8 + 2 clerical support	civilian	both
Dallas Police Department, Texas	mid-1970s	Police Intelligence Research Specialist	4	1 sworn, 3 civilian	no
Green Bay Police Department, Wisconsin	October 1997	Crime Analyst	1	civilian	no
Las Vegas Metropolitan Police Department, Nevada	1989	Crime Analyst	8	civilian	both
Lenexa Police Department, Kansas	1995	Community Policing	1	civilian	no
Lexington Police Department, Kentucky		Crime Analyst	2	civilian	occasionally
Lincoln Police Department, Nebraska	1977	Police Detective Sergeant Police Service Officer Office Assistant III	5	1 sworn and 3 civilian	no

TABLE 7.1 *(continued)*

Agency	Year Crime Analysis Began	Titles	Number of Staff	Sworn or Civilian	Interns or Volunteers
Mesa Police Department, Arizona	1993	Crime Analyst	4 and 1 supervisor + support staff	civilian	volunteers and prehire officers
Overland Park Police Department, Kansas	1993	Crime Analyst Manager Crime Analyst Assistant	3 + support staff (alarm coordinator)	civilian	volunteers (5) interns occasionally
Phoenix Police Department, Arizona	in development	Research Analyst Officer	2+ 2 statistical support aides	1 sworn 1 civilian	volunteers occasionally
Pierce County Sheriff's Department, Washington	1998	Crime Research Technician	3	sworn and civilian	volunteers, interns occasionally
Pinellas County Sheriff's Department, Florida	1989		9	sworn and civilian	volunteers occasionally
Portland Police Bureau–Tactical Operation Division, Oregon	early 1980s	Crime Analyst	6 + ½-time clerical	sworn	interns

Department	Year	Titles	Number	Type	Other
Richmond Police Department, Virginia	1991	Crime Analyst II, Principal Administrative Crime Analyst	7 + one supervisor	civilian	volunteers
Rochester Police Department, New York	mid-1970s	Lieutenant, Sergeant, Investigators, Police Officers	8 + 4 clerical support	sworn (civilian clerical)	both
Savannah Police Department, Georgia	1990	Management Analyst	2 (1 criminal intelligence, 1 information management)	civilian	interns occasionally
Scottsdale Police Department, Arizona	1995	Crime Analyst Unit Supervisor, Police Analyst, Police Support Specialists	4 + 2 paid PT interns, 1 volunteer	civilian	both
Winston-Salem Police Department, North Carolina	1970s	Senior Public Safety Information Analysts	3	sworn and civilian	no

type of position for a longer period of time, often for their entire careers. In addition, civilians may come at a lower salary than sworn officers. A common disadvantage to hiring civilian analysts is the reluctance of field officers and detective investigators to accept and trust civilians. Until the analyst has proven himself or herself, officers often are reluctant to share confidential data and information despite the analyst having the appropriate clearance.

Where can these "highly qualified" civilians be found? Some analysts are found already working in other capacities within the department. College interns, police officers, analysts from other fields, and military personnel are also good prospects for the position. Having a police background (especially within the given agency) can be especially beneficial, minimizing the "getting familiar with your jurisdiction" issue that is so very important for the analyst.

Sworn officers have much to offer a crime analysis unit. However, sworn officers often are placed in such "specialty positions" only for a few years before being transferred to another unit or back to the street. Furthermore, sworn personnel may be promoted at some point. Officers placed in crime analysis units as a temporary ("light duty") position are often of little benefit to units beyond copying, distribution, and other menial tasks. Taking the time to train them proves fruitless when they are transferred back to routine patrol after being deemed "fit for duty." Since modern crime analysis requires ongoing and intensive training, investing in civilians who are more likely to stay in the job makes sense.

These factors endanger the stability and consistency within the unit. In addition to the loss of the person who was either being trained or had been trained, there is always the question of whether or not the position will be filled. Budget cuts can often affect newer units and/or units not funded by grants.

Once the type of personnel is determined, the number of analysts will become an issue. Larger cities have units of fifteen to twenty analysts, while smaller cities have one person working on crime analysis issues as only part of their job duties. One to two analysts per 100 officers has become a standard in the field. This may vary depending on the amount of crime (i.e., incidents and/or reports) in the jurisdiction. A jurisdiction with a relatively high crime rate may need to employ an above average number of analysts, while a jurisdiction with significantly less than average crime may stick to the one-analyst-per-hundred-officer ratio. The main thing to consider when determining staff numbers is the workload expectations. Unfortunately, crime analysts are often hired by those who are unaware of the amount of work crime analysis takes and the ongoing skill building needed to achieve a standard of excellence.

Using Volunteers

Volunteers, now more than ever, have been recognized as a very underutilized but valuable source of personnel. Often, when we think of volunteerism in police work, we may picture wannabe cops, elderly men and women, or overzealous homemakers with too much time on their hands. We may think that these groups of people might be good only for running errands, copying large amounts of documents, or other menial tasks.

It is true that a significant number of volunteers are made up of homemakers, retired persons (including many in the law enforcement field), and college students, but the idea that they are best utilized for copying and distribution is probably incorrect. Rather, each volunteer should be evaluated through employment history, conversations with the volunteer by paid personnel and/or a volunteer coordinator, and observations of activity within the workplace to determine his or her skill levels in various capacities. Perhaps some volunteers may prefer to do menial work such as copying and distribution, while others seek to improve various skills, including those related to computers, analysis, and compilation of data/information. It is only through the assessment by paid personnel and/or a volunteer coordinator that the volunteer's desires, ambitions, and abilities can be determined and proper job duties assigned.

Before any of this takes place, however, the department will need to actively seek volunteers. There are many places where volunteers can be located and identified. Often police personnel units can contact volunteer organizations within the community to identify people who have already expressed a desire to serve in various capacities. Other "volunteer" groups such as Kiwanis, American Legion, sororities, and the Lions will allow guest speakers at their meetings. Police personnel can take advantage of this opportunity to seek out volunteer-oriented persons who might be willing to try an entirely new, unfamiliar field. A department in Maryland is very effectively utilizing a volunteer staff of retired National Security Administration employees to supplement staff.

Once an applicant has successfully completed the necessary steps to become "employed" by the department, the skills and abilities assessments can take place. Once complete, the volunteer can be assigned tasks. Be sure to completely explain each task, step by step. Especially for those volunteers unfamiliar with police slang, understanding police reports, administrative reports, commonly used acronyms, or even general correspondence can be challenging. As each task is successfully completed, additional tasks can be added as the volunteer becomes comfortable with the expectations and needs of the department or unit. Many police department crime analysis units report that volunteers are used for some or all of the following functions:

- Copying
- Distribution
- Creation of simple crime maps
- Creation of administrative reports
- Creation of crime bulletins/arrest reports
- Tracking volunteer hours
- Entering field-interview forms/cards (FIFs/FICs)
- Locating FIFs/FICs or reports not turned in for processing
- Working on special projects
- Representing the unit at various meetings (internal and external)
- Recruiting additional volunteers

Although volunteers are giving their time free of charge to the department, expectations such as maintaining a professional image, respecting the set rules and regulations, and obeying all privacy/confidential information issues is a must. Volunteers should be expected to act at the same professional level as paid personnel.

With the advent of the community-oriented policing philosophy and the desire for the public to become more involved in fighting crime, using citizen volunteers in the police department is a tremendous benefit. This movement toward community-oriented policing may be especially effective in crime analysis units staffed by civilians, who may be perceived as less intimidating to citizens. The concerns over staffing shortages, high crime rates, and keeping the public involved in their community are certainly addressed through this avenue.

Using Interns

Some crime analysis units supplement their staff with college interns. Sometimes agencies pay interns; sometimes unpaid interns are available. Grant funds are available in some agencies for paid internships. College interns can be good data-entry clerks, and may be helpful for special projects. Criminal justice interns may seem to be the best choice, but other students have specialized knowledge to lend to a crime analysis unit and should not be overlooked.

If a local university has a geography or Geographic Information Systems program, interns with GIS skills can be utilized to help an undertrained crime analysis staff improve GIS skills. GIS interns can work on special projects, such as historical crime trend analysis and mapping, freeing time for crime analysts to work on tactical analysis. These students may be assigned to special projects that the crime analysis staff is unable to undertake because of high workloads.

Interns from management information systems or information technology programs may help the crime analysis unit with database development, querying, and computer software skill building.

Journalism interns may bring creativity to bulletin development, and may be useful in developing better newsletters and bulletins. They generally have good research skills and thus can benefit a crime analysis unit with strategic analysis projects assistance.

Interns may be used to supplement staff in the same manner as volunteers are used. The same considerations for privacy issues apply to interns. Interns may be less effective than long-term volunteers because they generally work for only one semester. The time spent training them must be measured against the time of service to determine whether or not interns can meet some of your crime analysis needs.

Centralized versus Decentralized

If the jurisdiction has only one station, whether the analyst(s) will be centralized or decentralized is not an issue. Obviously the analyst will be in the same building as the officers, detectives, and command staff. When this is the case, the physical location of the analyst within the building itself is the issue. When multiple buildings (stations, locations, and so on) are involved, as is with larger jurisdictions, the decision to centralize or decentralize the crime analysis unit becomes an important issue.

There are certainly advantages and disadvantages to each. When the analysts are centralized in one location, they have the advantage of knowing what projects the other analysts are working on, thus often preventing duplication of efforts on the same or very similar projects. In addition, as the skill levels and knowledge bases of the analysts will differ, having them grouped in one location allows both direct and indirect training. As a problem is encountered, it can be presented to others for assistance. This is obviously done much more easily in person than over the phone or by e-mail.

Another advantage to centralizing crime analysis is to keep the output consistent. When several different divisions or sectors request crime statistics, the analysts can determine the format for the report and consistently prepare the report. This will allow the divisions/sectors to more easily compare the data they receive with one another during various meetings or other relevant forums. Along the same lines, keeping the analysts together also allows for consistency in requests for hardware and software. The old adage that two heads are better than one must also hold true when several heads are put together to determine the needs of the units. Obviously, the knowledge base of a group of analysts is more advantageous than information only known by one person and assists in developing institutional memory.

The biggest disadvantage to centralizing crime analysis is that it often drastically separates the analysts from one of their primary customers—the officers. It can be very difficult when officers must actively seek out the unit, determine which analyst they are working with, and relate requests and needs on specific projects, especially if the analysts do not know the officers or vice versa.

Decentralizing crime analysis units has many advantages. Keeping analysts in all the stations, including substations, allows the line personnel easy access to their analysts. They are able to see and interact with the analysts on a daily basis. The analysts are more likely to be able to attend roll calls and take part in ride-alongs. Decentralization allows for the sworn officers at the station to become more familiar with the analysts and their capabilities and skills. It promotes the idea of working as a team, which is consistent with the community-oriented policing and problem-solving philosophy. Most important, however, it allows the analyst to stay current with his or her officers' specific needs, projects, assignments, and so on, as well as become familiar with localized problems.

The biggest disadvantage to decentralizing crime analysis units is the lack of consistency in supervision, direction, and output. Whereas one analyst may be putting 110 percent into each project, delivering on time and in a professional format, another station's analyst may simply be getting by, doing the minimum, or not completing requests. When the latter type of analyst is not monitored, officers can lose confidence in crime analysis and its benefits. When a replacement analyst arrives, it may take twice or three times as long to regain the officers' trust and confidence.

There is argument that the best alternative for larger agencies is a combination of centralized and decentralized crime analysis. By maintaining a group of analysts at headquarters while placing an analyst in each of the substations, agencies can reap the benefits of both philosophies. Although some of the decentralization issues (lack of supervision and consistency in output) are still present, the advantages of having both types may outweigh that disadvantage. Some larger agencies choose to place civilian analysts at headquarters, where they primarily target administrative crime analysis issues, while sworn officers are decentralized into the substations, working closely with beat officers on tactical and strategic issues. Assigning centralized analysts to different units or areas can also be an effective measure in workload distribution.

Physical Placement of the Unit Within the Agency

The crime analysis unit (or individual crime analyst, as it may be) should, without question, be placed as close to line personnel and investigations personnel as possible. The primary duties of an analyst are to perform administrative, strategic, and tactical crime analysis. Although most administrative crime analysis will be requested by command staff, a great deal of tactical and strategic crime analysis will be performed for the beat officers and detectives.

Administrative crime analysis should consist primarily of automated reports such as comparing this month to last or this year to last. Little direct, daily contact with administrators is needed to support administrative crime analysis. In addition, although timeliness is important to the data, the analyst is limited as to the amount of this type of analysis that can be done, especially toward the end of the month when the analyst is simply waiting for time to pass to allow the data to be gathered and compile the monthly reports.

Strategic and tactical analysis, on the other hand, requires the analyst to be very timely and in direct contact with the officers taking the reports and the detectives investigating them. Open lines of communication among all the parties involved in collecting, collating, and analyzing the data will be pertinent to disseminating timely and accurate data on which the officers can act. Feedback from the officers and detectives as to the usefulness of the information provided by the analyst can be received on a one-to-one basis, thus allowing the analyst to alter the information or methods of dissemination according to the needs of the customer.

If the unit is placed with or near administrative offices, such as planning and research, internal affairs, the chief's office, or in out-of-the-way locations, the analysts are much *less* likely to have ongoing interactions with their customers. This not only impedes traffic flow in and out of the unit but also can virtually stop it.

If an analyst finds himself or herself placed in this type of situation with no hope of moving to another location, he or she will want to seek ways of getting more foot traffic into the unit. This can be done by having fresh coffee available during the day, setting out candy or other treats for the officers, or simply calling and inviting an officer or officers to come on a certain day at a certain time. While the customers are in the area, the analyst will have more opportunities to interact with them, including presenting new ideas, new technologies, and new projects he or she is working on, thus showing the capabilities of crime analysis to potential customers.

Staff Interactions

Regardless of the location of the unit, the analyst will have many other opportunities to interact with customers. Some examples of these opportunities include participating in ride-alongs, attending roll calls and team meetings, and chance meetings in the hallway or lounge. A crime analyst should take advantage of every opportunity to interact with customers. During ride-alongs, an analyst can accomplish several positive tasks including: getting to know the officers and what their needs are; finding out what projects the officers are working on while giving information on how the crime analysis unit can assist; becoming more familiar with the officers' beats and the geography of the area; receiving direct feedback on CAU products and methods of dissemination; learning about the data collection process; and seeing the problems encountered by the officers in gathering the data.

Roll calls are another excellent way to interact with customers. Again, beyond having personal interaction with the officers, the analyst also has an opportunity to develop a sense of the team's mission and goals. Furthermore, the analyst may be allowed to take a few minutes out of roll call to update the officers on new technology and products being developed (or recently made available) to the officers. This is also an excellent time to teach (or reteach) the officers map reading or report writing. The analyst may have an opportunity to constructively express to the officers what needs the CAU has regarding reports that are and are not being met. For example, the officers may consistently neglect to include the name of an apartment complex in their reports. The analyst can stress the importance of this type of information to the officers, explaining why this information is necessary. Be sure to spend time complimenting the officers as well though, so that each time you "appear" in roll call, they do not have the impression that they are about to be criticized.

CRIME ANALYSIS UNITS ON THE WEB

To help the new crime analysis unit with ideas about how other agencies work, listed here are the Internet Web sites of a number of crime analysis units. Visit these Web sites to get a general idea of how other crime analysis units operate.

- Tempe, Arizona, Crime Analysis Unit
  <www.tempe.gov/cau>
- Cambridge, Massachusetts, Crime Analysis Unit
  (This site actually has current crime patterns listed for anyone to read.)
  <www.ci.cambridge.ma.us/~CPD>
- Scottsdale, Arizona, Crime Analysis Unit
  <http://www.scottsdaleaz.gov/lawenforcement/CrimeAnalysis/Default.asp>

- Garland, Texas, Police Department
  <http://www.ci.garland.tx.us/police/gpdca1.htm>
- Redding, California, Crime Analysis Unit
  <http://reddingpolice.org/rpd/rpdcau.html>
- Norman, Oklahoma, Crime Analysis Unit
  <http://www.ci.norman.ok.us/police/crime_analysis.htm>
- Boulder, Colorado, Crime Analysis Unit
  <http://www.electroactive.com/clients/bpd/2/>
- Mesa, Arizona, Crime Analysis Unit
  <http://www.ci.mesa.az.us/police/crime_analysisdefault.asp>
- Chandler, Arizona, Crime Analysis Unit
  <www.chandlerpd.com/cpd__site/crime_statistics/crime_stats_main.htm>
- Dallas, Texas
  <http://www.dallaspolice.net/index.cfm>
- Phoenix, Arizona
  <http://www.ci.phoenix.az.us/police/crista1.html>
- Sacramento, California, Neighborhood Crime Statistics, Crime Maps
  <www.sacpd.org>
- Washington County, Oregon, Sheriff's Department
  <http://www.co.washington.or.us/cgi/sheriff/lec.pl>
- Minneapolis, Minnesota, Police Department
  <http://www.ci.minneapolis.mn.us/citywork/police>
- Chesapeake, Virginia, Police Department
  <http://www.chesapeake.va.us/services/depart/police/police/index.shtml>
- Arizona Department of Public Safety
  <www.dps.state.az.us>

"MARKETING" AND FUNDING CRIME ANALYSIS

Marketing Crime Analysis: Achieving Credibility

"Selling" crime analysis to your local law enforcement agency may seem strange to a newcomer. After all, they hired you to do a job, so why does the agency need to be reminded of how useful your products are in the fight against crime?

Consider the following quote when marketing crime analysis:

Physicians are trained to diagnose a patient—*before* initiating a medical intervention. Good mechanics figure out what's really wrong with a car's motor—*before* they start replacing engine parts. Professional football teams utilize scouts—*before* the players take the field—to gather information that will improve the team's chance of winning. Should we plan and carry out law enforcement operations in ignorance? (Porter 1997, 27)

In the following contribution,* crime analyst Mel Rhamey, from Boulder, Colorado, offers an interesting story on how difficult it can be to achieve credibility in the crime analysis field, and how important it is to strive to obtain it.

"Crime Analysis Success—Fighting the Credibility Battle"

In order to be an effective crime analyst, it is necessary to go to battle to establish credibility within your agency. Often you will win the battle, but the war will go on. It is a long and frustrating process.

Eighteen years ago, when I began my career as the crime analyst for the Boulder Police Department in Boulder, Colorado, I already had three strikes against me. I was very young, I was female (in what was then a completely male-dominated profession), and I had virtually no law enforcement experience. Armed with a master's degree in public administration, a six-month internship in planning and research at the police department, and the enthusiasm of youth, I initially believed that just landing the position was the highest hurdle I would have to traverse. It was not long before I discovered how wrong I was.

There is a lengthy and complicated learning process that must be mastered. In order to function, it is necessary for the analyst to learn both the external environment and the internal environment. Therefore, I had to learn not only everything about Boulder, Colorado, much as a new officer must do, but also everything about the political workings of the department, its particular culture, and the day-to-day human interactions. This "psychological study," if you will, was much more difficult than obtaining the "street" knowledge and took much longer. Once I had somewhat of a grasp of both environments, I still found that establishing credibility was a slow and painful process and had to be accomplished on almost a one-to-one basis.

After five years as the crime analyst, I still encountered what I like to refer to as the "head-patting syndrome." This happens when you approach a detective or an officer with some of the greatest information ever produced, something that will probably solve at least a half dozen cases, result in the incarceration of some

---

*Printed with permission from Mel Rhamey.

notorious bad guy, and make you all national heroes. But what happens? You get a pat on the head, a patronizing smile, and you are sent on your way. If you stop and look back, you may even get a chance to see all your hard work deposited in the circular file cabinet, next to the recipient's desk. Of course, this particular syndrome is preferable to the "If you want to tell me something about crime, spend twenty years in a patrol car" reaction, which also is something many new crime analysts are often faced with and a statement I had heard on more than one occasion. Frankly, I have personally known several officers who spent twenty years in a patrol car and by all appearances they must never have gotten out of the car, because they really knew very little about crime.

As time went on, I made inroads with some people and my hard work and enthusiasm slowly began to pay off. Then came the *big break.* Given enough time and perseverance, something will occur in each analyst's life when some analytic revelation rockets him or her into the next phase of the career. This is how it happened for me.

I had been following a series of residential burglaries that were occurring in the Mapleton Hill neighborhood in Boulder. They were unusual because the burglar was taking very little from the home. If cash was in plain view it was taken, but otherwise it appeared as though the burglar was just looking around the house. The other outstanding element to these burglaries was the fact that the exterior porch lights were often unscrewed. After several weeks the burglaries stopped, but we had a sexual assault occur in the neighborhood. The suspect broke into the victim's home and his MO included cutting the phone wires and unscrewing the light bulb on the lamp next to her bed. I immediately believed that the burglaries were related to the sex assault. The burglar was in fact a rapist, searching for a victim. He finally had found one.

Two weeks after the rape, we received a prowler call from an area south of where the burglaries and sex assault had occurred. Officers arrived immediately and arrested a male who had cut the screen on an open window. The resident was a lone female. The male appeared extremely intoxicated and said he thought he was at his house, but the arresting officer noted that by the time the suspect was booked into the jail, no signs of intoxication existed. Two days later, the victim in the prowler call made a supplemental phone report to the arrest. She said she didn't know if it meant anything, but her porch light had been unscrewed. When I read that report, all the hair on the back of my neck stood up. I knew the burglar was a rapist and now I had a name. When I checked field interview cards for the arrested prowler, I found two contacts with him in early a.m. hours, both in the neighborhood where the activity was occurring. In each of these contacts, he acted drunk, and said he was on his way home. It was his standard way of dealing with a police contact. I put all the information together and presented it to the detective assigned. I got a smile and a pat on the head.

A month later, we had a second rape—same MO. I went back to the assigned detective and asked if he had checked out the suspect I had given him. He had not. He showed me a few names of people he was looking at and said he would get around to my suspect "one of these days." I took my information to his sergeant, who said, "This is very interesting, be sure Detective Mudd [name changed to protect the idiot] gets a copy." I decided to send a copy of my report to the division chiefs and the chief of police. This, of course, was not how the chain of command worked and I was taking a big risk, but I was not willing to sit back and allow the list of victims to grow when I was 99.9 percent certain I knew who the suspect was. I survived this breach of protocol because the chief agreed with me. My suspect was using an alias and his only criminal history was a traffic-related arrest with our agency. When his prints were submitted to the FBI, his real identity was determined and he previously had served time for sexual assault.

By now he had found a third victim, but we were unable to find him. A task force had been formed and a saturation patrol was assigned to the Mapleton Hill area I had targeted. For two months nothing happened. Then the suspect committed forcible rapes on back-to-back nights, dropping his wallet at the scene of the last assault. There was no question now; I had identified the correct suspect. He was located, arrested, charged, and convicted for five first degree sex assaults and sentenced to eighteen years in the department of corrections.

I have had numerous successes over the last eighteen years, some more glamorous than this, but I will never forget the one that finally broke down that credibility barrier. From the day that rapist's wallet was recovered, I never again suffered the "head-patting syndrome" or heard the "twenty years in a patrol car" line. I still encounter a nonbeliever on occasion, but it generally does not take long to make him or her a convert. After all, that detective who would not check out my suspect? His name was Mudd.

Marketing crime analysis involves understanding your agency's needs for crime analysis tools, developing the relevant tools, educating the users of these tools, and tracking the successes.

Funding

Most crime analysis units experience the frustration of knowing that there is so much more they could do, but cannot, because of inadequate resources to undertake any additions to current workloads.

Some agencies started their crime analysis units with grant money, and when the grant expired, committed to hiring crime analysts as part of the regular operating budget. Grant money through the federal government Community Oriented Policing Services, the Law Enforcement Block Grant, and other initiatives have been used to help create crime analysis functions by purchasing equipment, paying for staffing on a time-limited basis, and paying for training needs.

In addition, it may be possible to obtain equipment and other resources for crime analysis from private foundations; it is something to consider. It is extremely important to work with your agency within the parameters of their rules and regulations when attempting to find alternative funding sources.

*Web Sites with Grant Information Through the U.S.
Department of Justice*

- U.S.-DOJ Bureau of Justice Assistance (Grants)
  <http://www.ojp.usdoj.gov/fundopps.htm>
- U.S.-DOJ "COPS" Grants
  <http://www.cops.usdoj.gov>
- U.S.-DOJ Grants
  <http://www.usdoj.gov/10grants/index.html>

Web Sites for Grant Writing and Grantsmanship

- National Network of Grantmakers
  <http://www.nng.org/>
- The Grantsmanship Center
  <http://tgci.com>

Web Sites of Foundations

- Council on Foundations
  <http://www.cof.org>
- The Chronicle of Philanthropy
  <http://www.philanthropy.com/>

State public safety offices also provide grant funding and should be explored for availability of money to meet agency crime analysis needs.

HOW DO WE MEASURE SUCCESS?

Many crime analysis units do not have a formal mechanism in place for measuring success. Reliance on informal feedback from officers and police managers to guide crime analysts often is the primary method for practitioners to measure success. Developing formal means to assess the functions of crime analysis is important for those who want to advocate for more staffing, funding, and management support for crime analysis.

Agencies formally measure the success of their crime analysis units in a number of ways.

- Lower crime rates as a result of implementing crime analysis in an agency
- Higher clearance rates leading to the apprehension of suspects attributed to information crime analysts supply
- Customer satisfaction surveys (Johnson 1999)
- Regular meetings with staff for feedback
- Measuring productivity of analysts
- Interdepartmental assessment surveys
- Anecdotal "success stories"
- Documentation of instances where crime analysis information assisted in the apprehension of a suspect or otherwise helped resolve a community crime problem

Undoubtedly other means can measure success. One of the challenges for the future of crime analysis is the development of objective means and methods to assess the value and use of knowledge obtained through crime analysis in law enforcement.

The Los Angeles County Sheriff's Department's Crime Analysis Program has developed a comprehensive annual report that measures productivity through tracking requests, counting number of products provided, and results. In measuring results, the agency reports an eleven-year (1987-1998) cumulative total of 115,627 requests for crime analysis services; 54,345 products created; 55,524 series/patterns identified; 3,212 suspects identified; 2,879 suspects arrested; 5,643 cases cleared; 1,920 property identifications; $5,546,137 in property recovered; and $202,845,630 in narcotics seized (Los Angeles County Sheriff's Department 1999). This type of tracking effort requires continual communication between the crime analysis unit and end-users, but such tracking clearly measures success and can prove the tangible benefits of crime analysis.

CRIME ANALYSIS SUCCESS STORIES

Next, a few crime analysis success stories are provided from working analysts to give you a flavor of what qualifies as success in the field.

Chief Tom Casady, Lincoln, Nebraska

My favorite of recent vintage is the identification of a pattern of sex offenses—indecent exposure and a single sexual assault of a nine-year-old boy—occurring in and around Wilderness Park in southwest Lincoln. We identified a diffuse trend over an eighteenth-month period with a similar MO and suspect description. This led to a surveillance project and the arrest of the perp—a convicted sex offender living about a mile away. We caught him about a year ago in the park with his pants off—literally. He is now awaiting trial for the sexual assault.

Dan Helms, Las Vegas, Nevada

Crime analysis has been intimately involved in support of several serial crime task forces. In more than one instance, we have successfully provided forecasting information which has assisted in the interception of a crime series. We have made many more substantial contributions to investigations. We have also provided support for prosecutorial courtroom presentations in a variety of cases. In one interesting serial crime task force use of GIS, the crime analyst created a flexible, optimized massive response plan which allowed an incident commander to successfully coordinate the actions of more than 250 officers to "swarm" a predicted serial crime event. This technique allowed the incident commander to initiate a meticulously crafted deployment plan with minimal risk to the public, maximum efficiency, and with a response time of less than thirty seconds.

Anne Gunther, Hampton, Virginia

Successes relating to the self-initiated tracking and identification of suspects have been many. The following three examples are particularly noteworthy.

First, an informant provided investigators with alias information on two possible homicide suspects. The information was researched through old and new computer systems with negative results. However, one of the aliases was located in the analyst's self-initiated and "antiquated" three-by-five card file. The name of this subject was familiar to the analyst because of past criminal activity. Although the information on the possible suspect was not well accepted, it proved to be accurate and the suspect was identified and arrested. The crime was later ruled accidental and not a homicide.

Second, the victim of a maiming noted that he thought the suspect had, at one time, resided at the location of the maiming. Field interview and arrest information was researched with a concentration on home addresses. Based on locating a subject with his home address being the same (even though it had been eight months before the incident took place), and the fact that his descriptors were similar, investigators were provided the information and were able to make an arrest.

Finally, through the combined efforts of a citizen providing an anonymous tip to Crime Line, watchfulness on the part of midnight shift officers, and the interrogation process, a smash-and-grab suspect was arrested and charged with numerous commercial burglaries. Synopsis: The analyst took a Crime Line call regarding the identity of the subject who had committed a "robbery" of a commercial establishment. It was known that the robbery was actually a burglary (citizens often use the incorrect terminology). There had been several with the same MO. The name was researched and it was learned through the research that the subject had a girlfriend who lived in the vicinity of the burglary locations and he had previously committed the same type of act. The subject rode a bicycle and the items stolen were easy-to-carry entertainment items. After the bulletin was disseminated, the subject was field interviewed. He was arrested.

Doug Rains, Aurora, Colorado

Over a period of a couple weeks, I identified what appeared to be an emerging crime pattern involving car break-ins at apartment complexes. The pattern was occurring within a four-hour period on only Sunday and Monday nights at apartment complex parking lots that backed up to greenbelt areas. I wrote a pattern report, which included an action plan, and gave it to the patrol commander. The commander took action by assigning a team of two uniformed officers to "stake out" the parking lot that I had projected to be the next target. On the first night out, the team observed a young man climbing over the privacy fence separating the apartment parking lot from the adjacent greenbelt. The subject looked around, approached a parked vehicle and pulled a screwdriver from his pocket. He then pried the driver side wing vent and stuck his arm through the opening to unlock the door. While his arm was still inside the victim's vehicle, the officers came up behind him and arrested him. He nearly fainted with surprise. After the arrest, the break-in pattern ended.

The second story involves a robbery pattern. We were having a rash of robberies at dry cleaning establishments. The suspect description was the same in each one; he wore a Halloween mask. The suspect seemed to be getting bolder with each robbery. No solid pattern existed for day of week or geographic location but all the robberies occurred within a one-hour period of the day. I did a projection (forecast) as to where and when the next likely robberies would occur. The projection was based on the suspect's tendencies rather than a tight pattern. The SWAT team and robbery unit supervisors were given the projection report. They took action by conducting surveillance on the two most likely dry cleaning locations identified in the report. The first day produced no results. However, on the second day the SWAT team observed an individual matching the general physical description of the suspect approach the cleaners at the projected time. Just as he reached for the door to enter, he pulled a Halloween mask from under his coat, put it on and entered the business. From their surveillance point, the SWAT team had the business covered in a matter of seconds. When the suspect exited the cleaners, he was arrested immediately outside on the sidewalk without incident. With his arrest, the pattern ceased.

Both of these operations resulted in great personal satisfaction for me—not to mention an increased credibility for crime analysis. Not all projections materialize but it is a crime analyst's job to make forecasts and suggest action plans to commanders when sufficient data dictates.

Sergeant Mark Stallo, Dallas, Texas

A number of successes have taken place as a result of using crime analysis information. In 1992, the crime analysis team looked at a string of grocery robberies and forecasted the location and date of the next robbery. The suspects were arrested and the robberies were cleared.

In the mid-1990s, the city of Dallas had a series of robberies that occurred in the driveways of affluent citizens. The detectives and crime analyst in our North Central Division plotted the locations the victims had frequented prior to each robbery and where they lived. They found that they had to cross two major intersections. They calculated the day and time that the next robbery would occur and deployed in those two intersections. Within an hour or two they made an arrest.

In 1997, we looked at where parolees lived in relation to where some sexual assaults were occurring. We found a parolee who fit the description, was released the day before the first crime occurred, lived in the apartment complex of one of the victims, and was pawning stolen property from four victims. Multiple life sentences.

Al Johnson, Austin, Texas

Probably our biggest success has been the complete overhaul and redesign of the Information Technology (IT) structure from a stand-alone one to a completely integrated network environment. Some other improvements include

- the implementation of a networked database;
- all analysts running ArcView from a quad processor server;
- obtaining two servers solely dedicated to crime analysis;
- obtaining Analysts' Notebook and setting it up to run from a server;
- increasing staffing from three to the current nine analysts;
- transition of a paper-only apartment and neighborhood association crime report to an interactive searchable Internet database;
- the standardization of all products produced by the unit;
- reorganization of a daily operational procedure, which resulted in time savings of three hours per day;
- selection and subsequent publication of a successful analysis in the *Crime Mapping Case Studies: Success in the Field,* Volume II (La Vigne and Warfell 2000); and
- honorable mention for our submission in the crime mapping competition for the 1999 International Crime Mapping Conference.

Michelle Arneson, Green Bay, Wisconsin

A community police officer was having problems with a bar in his area. We spent a lot of time putting together information on the number of calls there, how many officers on each call, what it was costing the city, how their volume compared to other bars in the area, and so on. It was very effective and we shut down the bar.

Lieutenant Thomas Evans, Pinellas County, Florida

Our Robbery Unit/Crimes Against Property Unit used the chapter's analysis reports in several significant cases. One case involved a series of regional armed robberies involving restaurants. In this case, the analysis aided in obtaining complete confessions from the robbery suspects who previously denied involvement in the crimes. The detective invited the analyst to sit in the debriefing interview after the suspect confessed. The analyst was able to refresh the suspect's memory on a number of cases.

The second case involved armed robberies of local pizza delivery shops. In this instance, the analyst produced a forecast of the day, date, time, and location of the next robbery. I am pleased to say the detectives' surveillance of the business, based on the forecast, resulted in the suspect's arrest.

In a third case, an analysis of a residential burglary series suggested that the perpetrator was using the public bus system for transportation. Based on the analyst's suggestion detectives conducted a surveillance of bus stops in the forecasted target area. Although another lead led to the suspect's arrest, during his confession to the crimes, he admitted to using the county bus system for transportation and on his last bus trip to commit a burglary he spotted detectives' surveillance and got back on the bus. We have many more successes like these.

Brian Cummings, Richmond, Virginia

One Richmond crime analyst identified a pattern of commercial robberies in the downtown area of the city of Richmond in 1996. The robberies started with one in January 1996 followed by one in February, two in March, and none in April. Between May 5 and May 7, there was one each day. The robberies continued to occur with greater frequency through the month of May. The analyst had issued several reports during this time. The analyst identified physical descriptions along with various MOs. The analyst also included information obtained from a sergeant at Third Precinct concerning a possible suspect with a similar physical description. One of the MOs that was identified was that one location was targeted only on the weekends (Friday through Sunday) on the evening/midnight shift. This location was near a major hotel and conference center. The analyst pointed out that the robberies were in an area that would allow the suspect an easy get-away route and that some of the locations had been targeted more than once. It was also noted that the suspect would leave the scene in a northerly direction. Investigation subsequent to the capture of the suspect revealed that the suspect lived to the northwest of the downtown area. The detectives used the information provided by the analyst to set up surveillance and an apprehension was made. The subject was arrested and turned out to be the same individual about whom the sergeant from Third Precinct had provided information during the investigation.

Gerald Tallman, Overland Park, Kansas

Overland Park was hit with a marked increase of residential burglaries of garages accessed through open garage doors. These "garage shopping" incidents were primarily centered in the southern half of our city. In a unified effort of crime analysis, crime mapping, patrol, investigations, and Community Oriented Policing and Problem Solving (COPPS), we were able to successfully educate our citizens to keep their garage doors closed and locked, and in a short time frame were able to almost eliminate these incidents. In a speech on crime mapping and technology, then U.S. Attorney General Janet Reno publicly praised our use of technology and cooperative policing efforts in combating this problem.

Chapter 8

Education and Training Resources

OVERVIEW

It is clear to anyone looking into this field that crime analysis education and training opportunities are very limited at the present time. Many individuals already working as crime analysts expect that more courses and hands-on training will be developed by universities and agencies as appreciation for the benefits of systematic crime analysis by well-trained crime analysts increases. Meanwhile, this book provides information on most of the education and training options currently available for crime analysts at the local law enforcement level in the United States. Since it is expected that more training resources will be developed after the publication of this book, we suggest that readers search the Internet for other training options.

The Royal Canadian Mounted Police have established an understudy program for criminal intelligence analysts that might serve as a good model for the future training of all law enforcement analysts. It is called the Criminal Intelligence Analyst Understudy Program and consists of three major components involving approximately two years' training. This is vastly superior to the training offered to most analysts in any organization, and was developed because the RCMP recognized that the two to three weeks of training provided to most analysts was woefully inadequate.

Candidates must pass specified objectives and work under the direction of a tutor/mentor. The trainees are screened carefully, oriented thoroughly to the Intelligence Program, and undergo concurrent required training in a variety of analyses (including intelligence analysis, strategic analysis, computer courses, effective presentation, instructional techniques, and specialized courses). From the second to eighteenth month of the program, trainees receive on-the-job training

in analytical report writing, presentation exercises, and other specialty studies. In the nineteenth to twenty-third month of the program, trainees learn the elements of law and courts as applied to analytical work, such as giving expert testimony and presentation of
evidence (Fahlman 1998).

It is important for the future of crime analysis as a profession that
police managers and educators realize the need for in-depth and ongoing training for both crime and intelligence analysts. The nature of
analytical work requires that analysts receive training to use state-of-
the-art software and stay abreast of innovations in the analytical and
information-processing field. New, more effective tools for analysis
are being invented right now, this very moment. Analysts of the future must be able to use whatever tools exist if they are to do their jobs
effectively. Constant, rapid change is a fact of our society. In the war
against crime, we must use all the equipment and resources we have
effectively. Ongoing training for crime analysts is not a luxury; it is a
necessity.

TRAINING OPTIONS FOR THOSE EMPLOYED
IN LAW ENFORCEMENT

The Alpha Group

Most crime analysts in North America have heard of Steve Gottlieb, the executive director of the Alpha Group—he is considered by
many to be the guru of crime analysis. Mr. Gottlieb teaches a week-
long course called Crime Analysis Applications, which is conducted
in locations all over North America, as well as in Europe. Mr. Gottlieb's class comes highly recommended, and often has been the only
such training available for those just entering the field, as well as for
those who have been analyzing crime for years.

The Alpha Group offers other courses for crime analysts and any
other law enforcement personnel who would like to benefit from improving crime analysis skills. Listed following with a brief description, are three courses relevant to crime and intelligence analysts:

- Crime Analysis Applications Training—A basic, comprehensive, thirty-six-hour course in crime analysis covering opera-

tional issues in starting a crime analysis unit, analyzing crime, and statistical processes.

- Criminal Investigative Analysis Training—A forty-hour course in identifying the physical, behavioral, and personality characteristics of offenders who commit rape and homicide, with an emphasis on serial offenders.
- Criminal Intelligence Analysis Training—A thirty-six-hour course in developing and using intelligence at the investigative level, the departmental level, and at the central or regional level.

For more information contact:
The Alpha Group
P.O. Box 8
Montclair, CA 91763
909-989-4366
909-476-6810 Fax
<www.alphagroupcenter.com>
E-mail Steve Gottlieb: <crimecrush@aol.com>

By taking these courses, individuals can earn continuing education units (CEUs) from California State University, which may be applied to the Certificate Award in Crime and Intelligence Analysis. There are additional criteria for earning this credit; contact California State University, Sacramento, at 916-278-4547, for more information.

Anacapa Sciences

Anacapa Sciences has been offering analytical training for law enforcement since 1971, with a primary focus on intelligence analysis. Open courses are scheduled at various locations around the United States, and closed courses are available for agencies with a need to train larger numbers of individuals. Anacapa courses serve as the foundation of training for most intelligence analysts. Courses include Criminal Intelligence, Analysis, Analytical Investigation Methods, Financial Manipulation Analysis, and Advanced (computer-aided) Intelligence Analysis. For more information contact:

Anacapa Sciences, Inc.
P.O. Box 519
Santa Barbara, CA 93102-0519

805-966-6157, ext. 10
805-966-7713 Fax
<www.anacapasciences.com>
E-mail: <BAGates@anacapasciences.com>

The International Association of Chiefs of Police

Training in crime analysis by practicing crime analysts is offered at various locations by the International Association of Chiefs of Police. For information contact:

1-800-THE-IACP
<http://www.theiacp.org>

The Michigan Regional Community Policing Institute

A Crime and Data Analysis Workshop is offered by the Michigan Regional Community Policing Institute. It is a one-day workshop with a fee. Other types of law enforcement training are offered by this agency. For information contact:

Michigan Regional Community Policing Institute
1-800-892-9051 or 517-355-9648
517-432-0727 Fax
<www.cj.msu.edu/⌒outreach/rcpi/train.html>
E-mail: <weber@pilot.msu.edu>

The Carolinas Institute for Community Policing

The Carolinas Institute for Community Policing is a regional community policing institute offering GIS courses for crime analysis and community policing. Other training options are offered by this agency; contact them for more information on current offerings. For information contact:

Carolinas Institute for Community Policing
1750 Shopton Road
Charlotte, NC 28217
704-336-8549
704-336-8449 Fax
E-mail: <info@cicp.org>

Web-Based Training Options

- <http://www.letn.com>
  The Law Enforcement Television Network offers a variety of courses in videotape series and satellite transmissions.
- <http://www.mctft.com>; <http://www.rcta.org/>
  Multijurisdictional Counterdrug Task Force training is available for law enforcement personnel working on drug task forces or drug investigative units. Distance learning courses are available in topics such as analytical investigative techniques and criminal street gang identification.
- <http://www.apus.edy/amu/home.edu>
  The American Military University offers a graduate major in intelligence and an undergraduate course in this topic, with a national emphasis. It is a distance learning program.
- <http://nhac.org/training/calendar.htm>
  The High Intensity Drug Trafficking Area (HIDTA) program offers analytical training and training in software applications, as well as training to learn foreign languages.
- <http://www.cpc.gc.ca/>
  The Canadian Police College offers courses to employees of recognized Canadian Police Services. Training for police services out of Canada must be requested in writing by your police department to the Canadian Embassy to the attention of the Royal Canadian Mounted Police liaison officer. Courses include Intelligence Analysis and Strategic Intelligence Analysis. Internet-based courses offered through the Canadian Police College include topics such as analytical function, inductive reasoning, data evaluation, inference, matrix, link analysis diagrams, and report writing.
- <http://www.intstudycen.com>
  The Intelligence Study Center is based in Australia and specializes in strategic intelligence analysis training.
- <http://www.policetraining.net/>
  The Police Training Web site has up-to-date listings of seminars and distance learning opportunities, including crime analysis training.

- <www.fips.nw3c.org>
  The National White Collar Crime Center offers training in Internet-related crime analysis.
- <www.investigationtraining.com>
  The Investigation Training Institute
- <www.ustreas.gov/fletc>
  The Federal Law Enforcement Training Center offers a Criminal Intelligence Analyst Training Program.
- <www.nhac.org>
  The National High Intensity Drug Trafficking Area (HIDTA) Assistance Center offers a distance-learning training program on CD-ROM at no charge. Those completing and submitting an exam may receive a certificate for the course. Call: 305-716-3218.

Other Training Links

- <www.search.org> (Search)
- <www.infotech-europe.com> (InfoTech)
- <www.actnowinc.org> (ActNow, Inc.)
- <www.cactiis.com> (CACTiiS)
- <www.policefoundation.org> (Police Foundation)

Associations with Annual Training Conferences

- IACA—International Association of Crime Analysts
  <www.iaca.net>
- MACA—Massachusetts Association of Crime Analysts
  <www.macrimeanalysts.com>
- CCIAA—California Crime and Intelligence Analysts' Association
  <www.crimeanalyst.org>
- FCIAA—Florida Crime and Intelligence Analyst Association
  <www.fciaa.org>

EDUCATION AND TRAINING OFFERED BY COLLEGES AND UNIVERSITIES

California is the first state university system to develop a crime and intelligence analysis certification program. In California, successful completion of this program at one of the following universities allows candidates to apply to become certified crime and intelligence analysts, a credential from the California Department of Justice. All participants in the four programs listed are required to complete a 400-hour practicum in crime analysis at a law enforcement agency.

California State University, Sacramento
College of Continuing Education
3000 State University Drive East
Sacramento, CA 95819
916-278-4547
916-278-4602 Fax

University of California at Riverside
1200 University Avenue, Room 336
Riverside, CA 92507
909-787-5804
<www.unex.ucr.edu>

California State University, Fullerton
P.O. Box 6870
Fullerton, CA 92834-6870
714-278-2611
714-278-2088 Fax
<www.TakeTheLead.fullerton.edu>

Rio Hondo Community College in Whittier, California, offers a forty-hour, hands-on course called Crime Analysis Mapping Program. Contact:

Bob Feliciano
562-692-0921, ext. 705
<www.riohondo.edu/leo>
<bfeliciano@riohondo.edu>

George Mason University in Virginia offers a Professional Certificate in Crime Mapping and Analysis. There are three tracks in this program: one for law enforcement officers and administrators, one for crime analysts and coordinators, and one for database and system administrators. Contact:

> 703-993-8337
> <http://ocpe.gmu.edu/certificate_programs/crimemapping.html>
> <info@mail.ocpe.gmu.edu>

The Delaney Center for Public Sector Information at Mount St. Mary's College offers the Professional Certificate in Information Management/Analysis. This accredited certification program is designed to prepare students for analytical work currently required by both the law enforcement and intelligence communities. With five core required courses and two electives, focus is on gaining understanding of data analysis with an emphasis on proficient written and oral reporting, as well as basic research skills. Contact:

> Father Delaney Center for Public Sector Information
> Mount St. Mary's College
> Emmitsburg, MD 21727
> 301-447-3417
> <www.msmary.edu/cpsi>

The Criminal Justice and Legal Studies Department of the University of Central Florida offers a Graduate Certificate in Crime Analysis. It is intended for both traditional criminal justice students and practitioners, emphasizing utilization of available technologies to develop and perform crime analysis. The program requires a bachelor's degree or higher and consists of three courses totaling nine credit hours: Data Management Systems for Crime Analysis, Crime Mapping and Analysis, and Advanced Crime Mapping and Analysis. Contact:

> R. Cory Watkins, Assistant Professor
> Department of Criminal Justice and Legal Studies
> 4000 Central Florida Blvd.
> Orlando, FL 32816-1600
> 407-823-0365
> 407-823-5360 Fax
> <http://www.ucf.edu>
> <rwatkins@mail.ucf.edu>

Camden County College, in New Jersey, is in the process of developing a certification program in crime and intelligence analysis. The proposed program will consist of eight courses, including Crime Analysis, Criminal Intelligence Analysis, Criminal Investigative Analysis, Crime Mapping, Elements of Statistics I, Quantitative Research in Criminal Justice, Logic and Reason, and a controlled elective (selected with program coordinator). Requirements for admission specify that the applicant have a minimum two-year degree from an accredited institution, a minimum of sixty credit hours, or be practicing crime analysis meeting specified competency requirements. Incoming students must have completed courses in administration of justice, criminal law, criminal investigations, and personal computer applications or demonstrate a competency in these areas. For more information contact:

Professor Eugene Evans
Camden County College
115 Washington Avenue
Haddonfield, NJ 08033
856-227-7200, ext. 4623
<cjprof@comcast.net>

Mercyhurst College, in Erie, Pennsylvania, has a Research and Intelligence Analysis Program, geared primarily for training history majors to become intelligence analysts in government and business. Contact:

Robert Heibel
Mercyhurst College
501 East 38th Street
Erie, PA 16546-0001
814-824-2000
814-824-2219 Fax
<rheibel@mercyhurst.edu>

St. Joseph's University offers an MS degree—a criminal justice concentration in law enforcement intelligence and crime analysis. Contact:

St. Joseph's University
College of Arts and Sciences
Graduate Program in Criminal Justice
5600 City Avenue, MV 287
Philadelphia, PA 19131
<http://www.sju.edu/ACADEMIC_PROGRAMS/GRAD_ART_
SCIENCE/index.html>

Chapter 9

Other Resources

RECOMMENDED AGENCY RESOURCES

Regional Information Sharing Systems (RISS)
<http://www.iir.com/riss/>

RISS is a federally funded program to promote the sharing of intelligence and coordination of crime-fighting efforts across jurisdictions. Although its emphasis is on intelligence analysis and organized crime, the six regional centers that comprise RISS (which encompass all fifty states, two Canadian provinces, the District of Columbia, Australia, Guam, the U.S. Virgin Islands, and Puerto Rico) can be a resource for crime analysts at the local law enforcement level. Secure intranets help law enforcers network with the goal of sharing timely information. Analysis of multijurisdictional crime, information-sharing conferences, loans of equipment, and funds for investigations may be provided by RISS. For information contact:

Mr. Richard Revzan, Program Manager
State and Local Assistance Division
Bureau of Justice Assistance
810 Seventh Street, NW
Washington, DC 20531
202-305-2923
202-305-2543 Fax

The Six RISS Centers

1. Middle Atlantic-Great Lakes Organized Crime Law Enforcement Network (MAGLOCLEN): Includes Delaware, Indiana, Maryland, Michigan, New Jersey, New York, Ohio, Pennsylva-

nia, and the District of Columbia, and has member agencies in the Canadian provinces of Ontario and Quebec.

140 Terry Drive
Suite 100
Newtown, PA 18940
215-504-4910

2. Mid-States Organized Crime Information Center (MOCIC): Includes Illinois, Iowa, Kansas, Minnesota, Missouri, Nebraska, North Dakota, South Dakota, and Wisconsin, and has member agencies in Canada.

1610 East Sunshine, Suite 100
Springfield, MO 65804
417-883-4383

3. New England State Police Information (NESPIN): Includes Connecticut, Maine, Massachusetts, New Hampshire, Rhode Island, and Vermont, and has member agencies in Canada.

124 Grove Street, Suite 305
Franklin, MA 02038
508-528-8200

4. Regional Organized Crime Information Center (ROCIC): Includes Alabama, Arkansas, Florida, Georgia, Kentucky, Louisiana, Mississippi, North Carolina, Oklahoma, South Carolina, Tennessee, Texas, Virginia, and West Virginia, as well as Puerto Rico and the U.S. Virgin Islands.

545 Marriott Drive
Suite 850
Nashville, TN 37214
615-871-0013

5. Rocky Mountain Information Network (RMIN): Includes Arizona, Colorado, Idaho, Montana, Nevada, New Mexico, Utah, and Wyoming, and has member agencies in Canada.

2828 North Central Avenue
Suite 1000
Phoenix, AZ 85004-1027
602-351-2320

6. Western States Information Network (WSIN): Includes Alaska, California, Hawaii, Oregon, and Washington, and has member agencies in Canada, Australia, and Guam.

P.O. Box 903198
Sacramento, CA 94203-1980
916-263-1166

HIDTAs (High Intensity Drug Trafficking Areas)

HIDTAs are joint efforts of local, state, and federal law enforcement agencies designed to address drug problems in specific regions of the country. HIDTAs develop threat assessments, formulate strategies, develop and implement initiatives, and measure outputs and outcomes. The HIDTA Assistance Center offers training and resources to participants. If a crime analyst's agency falls within an HITDA area, he or she may benefit from accessing their resources. Contact:

HITDA Assistance Center
8401 NW 53rd Terrace, Suite 208
Miami, FL 33166
305-716-3270
305-716-3218 Fax
<http://www.nhac.org>

PERF (Police Executive Research Forum)

From the Web site:
The Police Executive Research Forum (PERF) is a national membership organization of progressive police executives from the largest city, county, and state law enforcement agencies. PERF is dedicated to improving policing and advancing professionalism through research and involvement in public policy debate.

PERF has created a bulletin board to encourage law enforcement agencies, practitioners, and academics to exchange information about issues they are encountering within their departments and communities as well as new practices in the field of policing. Conference topics on the WebBoard include technology, problem solving, training, and crime-specific problems. Contact:

Police Executive Research Forum (PERF)
1120 Connecticut Avenue
Suite 930
Washington, DC 20036
202-466-7820
202-466-7826 Fax
<http://www.policeforum.org/>

RECOMMENDED PUBLICATIONS

- *The Problem-Oriented Guide for Police Series* consists of a number of guidebooks available on topics such as robberies at ATMs, assaults in and around bars, and residential burglary. These publications are an informative resource for crime analysts, police officers, and citizens involved in community policing. Guidebooks are available online at <www.cops.usdoj.gov> or can be ordered in hard copies at 1-800-421-6770.
- The Crime Mapping & Analysis Program (CMAP), at the National Law Enforcement & Corrections Technology Center (NLECTC), Rocky Mountain Region (a program of the National Institute of Justice), offers the publication *Advanced Crime Mapping Topics*—the result of the first Advanced Crime Mapping Topics Symposium. Nineteen leading professionals and academicians in the fields of crime analysis, crime mapping, spatial analysis, and criminology joined together in Denver during June 2001, conducting an in-depth exchange of research findings and practical knowledge. These highly focused discussions and exciting exchanges have resulted in fifteen powerful and comprehensive articles. CMAP is pleased to offer these articles in a single, authoritative collection: *Advanced Crime Mapping Topics.* Sub-

jects include investigative analysis, problem solving, discrete site analysis, and resource allocation. Download your free copy of this on-screen publication in Adobe Portable Document File (PDF) format today, using the following link: <http://www.nlectc.org/cmap/cmapadvanced.html>

- Crime Reduction Toolkits offered online from the United Kingdom's Home Office can provide you with a number of ideas for addressing crime problems and analysis issues in your jurisdiction. <http://www.crimereduction.co.uk/toolkits/>

Other Publications of Interest

- Bureau of Justice Statistics' *Sourcebook Online*
  <http://www.albany.edu/sourcebook/>
- *Forecaster*
  (International Association of Crime Analysts members' bimonthly publication)
  <www.iaca.net>
- *Government Technology*
  <www.govtech.net>
- *IALEIA Journal*
  (International Association of Law Enforcement Intelligence Analysts members' quarterly journal)
  <http://www.ialeia.org/>
- *Intelligence Report* (Southern Poverty Law Center)
  <www.splcenter.org>
- *Law Enforcement Bulletin* (FBI)
  <http://www.fbi.gov/leb/leb.htm>
- *Law Enforcement Technology*
  <www.law-enforcement.com>
- *National Institute of Justice Journal*
  <www.ojp.usdoj.gov/nij/journals>
- *The Police Chief*
  <www.theiacp.org>

RECOMMENDED INTERNET SITES

- America's Most Wanted
  <http://www.amw.com>

- The Better Business Bureau
  <http://www.bbb.org/>
- Central Intelligence Agency
  <http://www.cia.gov>
- Companies Online Search
  <http://www.companiesonline.com>
- COPNET: Police Resource List
  <http://www.copnet.org>
- Database America People Finder
  <http://www.databaseamerica.com>
- Drug Enforcement Administration
  <http://www.usdoj.gov/dea/>
- FBI
  <http://www.fbi.gov>
- Federal Bureau of Prisons
  <http://www.bop.gov/>
- FedStats
  <http://www.fedstats.gov/>
- The 555-1212.com—Directory
  <http://www.555-1212.com>
- Illinois Criminal Justice Information Authority
  <http://www.icjia.state.il.us>
- Infoseek Guide
  <http://www.infoseek.com>
- InfoSpace—The Ultimate Directory
  <http://www.infospace.com>
- International Association of Chiefs of Police
  <http://www.theiacp.org>
- The International CPTED Association
  <http://www.cpted.net>
- International Fugitive
  <www.mostwanted.com>
- Internet Address Finder
  <http://www.iaf.net>
- The Internet Sleuth
  <http://www.isleuth.com>
- Investigative Resource Center Databases
  <http://www.factfind.com/database.htm>

- Investigator's Guide to Sources of Information
  <http://www.gao.gov/special.pubs/soi.htm>
- Investigator's Toolbox
  <http://pimall.com/nais/in.menu.html>
- Justice Research & Statistics Association
  <http://www.jrsainfo.org>
- LEXIS-NEXIS (cost involved)
  <http://www.lexis-nexis.com/>
- The National Address Server
  <http://www.cedar.buffalo.edu/adserv.html>
- National Criminal Justice Reference Service
  <http://www.ncjrs.org>
- National Fraud Information Center
  <http://www.fraud.org>
- The National Institute of Justice
  <http://www.ojp.usdoj.gov/nij>
- National Insurance Crime Bureau
  <http://www.nicb.com>
- National Sheriff's Association
  <http://www.sheriffs.org/>
- Office of Community Oriented Policing Services
  <http://www.cops.usdoj.gov>
- Police Foundation
  <www.policefoundation.org>
- The Police Officer's Internet Directory
  <http://www.officer.com>
- Reference.COM Search
  <http://www.reference.com>
- Research-It!
  <http://www.itools.com>
- SEARCH
  <http://www.ch.search.org>
- Sex Offender.Com
  <http://www.sexoffender.com>
- Social Statistics Briefing Room at the White House Web
  <http://www.whitehouse.gov/fsbr/ssbr.html>
- Telephone Directories of the World
  <http://www.globalyp.com/world.htm>

- U.S. Bureau of the Census
  <http://www.census.gov>
- U.S. Bureau of Justice Statistics
  <http://www.ojp.usdoj.gov/bjs>
- U.S. Bureau of Labor Statistics
  <http://stats.bls.gov>
- Virtual Librarian—links to many resources
  <http://www.virtuallibrarian.com/>
- Welcome to WhoWhere?
  <http://www.whowhere.com>
- The World Email Directory and other sourcs of e-mail addresses:
  <http://worldemail.com>
  <www.informus.com>
  <http://www.thecre.com/fedlaw/default.htm.>
  <http://www.search.org/it-clearinghouse/>

Appendix

Examples of Crime Analysis Products

Rochester Police Department
Crime Analysis Report

Auto Theft Analysis—End of Month Report
February 2000

Data Collection Status

An IMPACT query was run to find all reports with the Crime Context of "Stolen Vehicle," or Offense Description containing "Unauthorized Use" or "Auto Stripping," and the incident beginning date equal to or greater than 02/01/2000 but less than or equal to 02/29/2000. Using this query, 264 records were found.

The list was edited for duplicates and data entry errors. Five reports were also received but were not found in IMPACT. After this editing, the total number of reports reviewed at the time of this report was 219.

Statistical Data (City-Wide)

Of the 219 UUV reports reviewed by Crime Analysis, the following statistical analysis was made after review and reclassification. Three classifications are used but only those classified as "Legitimate Stolen Autos" will be analyzed in further detail.

Legitimate Stolen Autos

- 150 or 69 percent of the reports reviewed are legitimate stolen (or stripped) autos. (This number includes 6 attempted stolen vehicles, 5 vehicles that were stolen and then stripped, and 4 others that were stripped only.)

Statistical Data (City-Wide) *(continued)*

- 123 or 84 percent of these legitimate stolen autos have already been recovered at the time of this report.

- Several of the vehicles recovered were found to be involved in or targets of a secondary incident. They are as follows:

> 10 vehicles had been involved in MVA/H&Rs
> 3 vehicles had been set on fire (1 in Ontario Cty)
> 9 vehicles had been stripped (5 tailgates only, 1 with tailgate and plow stolen, 3 with doors taken)
> 1 vehicle had the interior door panels and rear seat removed
> 1 vehicle had the bumper removed
> 1 vehicle was taken during a robbery (Lake Section)

The most common vehicles stolen in February:

- Dodge Caravan—7 were stolen

Caravan SE

- Dodge Neon—5 were stolen

- Jeep Cherokee/Grand Cherokee—4 were stolen

- Dodge Spirit—4 were stolen

- Olds Delta 88—4 were stolen

Neon

Drug Related or Loaned out for Drugs

- 7 reports, or 3 percent of all reports reviewed were drug related

Other—Domestic, Suspect Otherwise Known, Unfounded, Other Circ.

- 62 reports or 28 percent of all reports reviewed were classified as "Other"

Stripped Vehicles

- As previously indicated, a total of 9 vehicles were stripped. This accounts for 6 percent of the total number of legitimate stolen vehicle reports filed this month.

Statistical Data— Section Specific

Legitimate Stolen Autos by Section

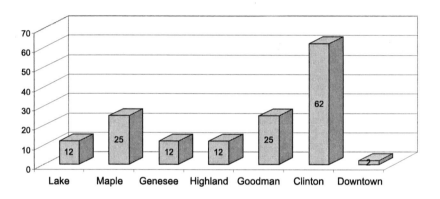

	Lake	Maple	Genesee	Highland	Goodman	Clinton	Downtown
# of Total Legitimate Stolens	12	25	12	12	25	62	2
# Recovered	9	22	10	11	22	51	2
% Recovered	75	88	83	92	88	82	100

	Lake	Maple	Genesee	Highland	Goodman	Clinton	Downtown
# Recovered for other agency	1	8	4	0	2	27	0

Recoveries for Other Agencies

42 vehicles were recovered for other law enforcement agencies.

Notable Incidents

- Several cases of auto stripping occurred this month and are related only in that they all involved the theft of vehicle doors from trucks (2 Chevys, 1 Dodge). The three incidents occurred in three different sections. Two of the thefts occurred without the vehicle being removed from the location. No other similarities were found.

- A dump truck was stolen from the Town of Irondequoit Highway Department and recovered on 2/28/00 in front of 185 Arbutus St. The plow had been stolen.

- Information was received and recently disseminated to coordinators regarding *John Doe #1*. He is suspected of continued thefts of vehicles and/or the theft of tires from vehicles in the city and county. He is said to be working with another unidentified M/B. His MO for stealing cars is to completely remove the lock from the vehicle door and then damage the column. When he steals tires, he does not bring a jack or blocks. He is said to find any available object and with the help of his accomplice, they lift the vehicle near a fender, thus shifting the weight of the vehicle to the other side. The object is then placed under the frame of the vehicle and it is lowered onto the object. Once a tire is removed, the vehicle is rocked from side to side to remove the other tires.

Patterns

This report indicates several cases of auto stripping involving the theft of tailgates from pickup trucks. This information was also mentioned in a previous February report. On 2/24/00, *John Doe #2* was arrested and charged with numerous thefts of plows and other property. Although only one tailgate has been recovered with this arrest, it is likely that *John Doe #2* was responsible for that pattern of thefts. The theft of tailgates has ceased since his arrest.

PIERCE COUNTY
W A S H I N G T O N
SHERIFF'S
DEPARTMENT
Crime Analysis and Information Unit

Armed Robbery Series Alert
February 24, 2000

BACKGROUND—An armed robbery series with unique characteristics has been underway since January 16, 2000. At least ten incidents have been identified to date. Most incidents have been in the Spanaway area, but the series has spilled into Lakewood and South Hill. The suspect favors gas station/convenience stores on major arterials and uses a black semiauto pistol. On one occasion the suspect fired rounds from the weapon into a display case. The majority of the incidents have occurred on weekend (Friday-Sunday) evenings, and ALWAYS between 1900-2200 hours.

There is a possibility that the suspect hit again Wednesday (February 23rd) on South Hill, however there are discrepancies in that case, including weapon (a knife was used), MO, and clothing. Det. Sgt. XXXXXXX is still investigating that case. A video review of that case DOES show a dark, bulky object tucked into the rear waistband of the suspect's pants. An additional robbery on Thursday, February 24th, at the Subway near 112th and Canyon is more likely to be the same suspect.

DESCRIPTION—The suspect has been described as an **Asian (and White and Hispanic) Male, with an age range between teens to mid 20s, thin, between 5'00" and 5'07" tall (See photos on page 3).** The clothing description varies, but a black stocking hat and a dark blue hooded sweatshirt have been described by several victims. He has been seen with a blue sweatshirt with the numerals "05" on the front in white.

APPROACH—On most of the incidents the suspect entered the store and picked up an item in the store before approaching the register area. Once at the register, the suspect offers money to pay for the item and waits until the cash register is opened before displaying the gun. After obtaining the money the suspect has fled out the door. Other than the incident on 2/23/00, there have been no getaway vehicles identified.

OTHER NOTES—The suspect has hit two separate stores on the same night on two occasions. Six of the nine incidents have occurred on Pacific Ave / SR7 between 152nd and 224th. He has hit the same store (Jackpot at 16521 Pacific Ave) two different times. If the suspect hits two different locations in an evening, the second location is a long distance away (South Hill to Spanaway, or Spanaway to Lakewood) from the first, but happens no more than 45 minutes later.

PROBABILITIES—If the suspect continues to operate as he has in the past, he is not likely to hit again until the range between 2/28 and 3/1—however, his favorite days in the past have been Friday and Sunday, so this weekend cannot be overlooked. The incident is very likely to occur between 1900 hours and 2200 hours. The first six incidents happened later in this time range, but the last four have been very close to 1900 hours. The primary area (noted above) extends from 152nd to 224th on Pacific Ave / Mtn. Hiway.

The map on the following page shows the nine known incidents. The labels show the sequence number of the incident and the day of the week.

If you have any additional information on this series, please e-mail Mike Carson in the Crime Analysis Unit.

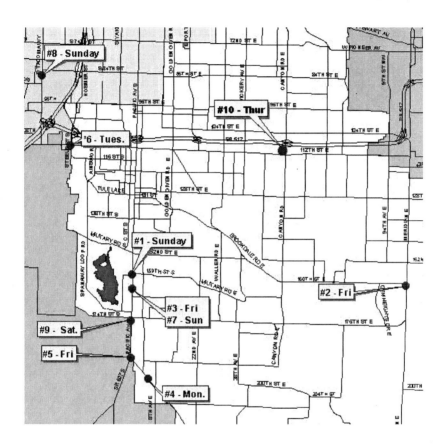

The photos on the next page are from the 1/21/00 robbery at the South Hill Texaco at 160th and Meridan

PINELLAS COUNTY SHERIFF'S OFFICE
CRIME ANALYSIS SECTION
INDECENT EXPOSURE SERIES
Squads 7 & 8 with Special Attention EVENING SHIFT
UPDATE – *NINE* EXPOSURE SEX ORGANS
April 13, 1999

(REF: 99-52787)
POSSIBLE SUSPECT: XXXXXXX W/M, 03/27/65, 6-00, 196, short straight brown receding hair, blue eyes, clean shaven, medium complexion, medium build, employed by XXXXXX, previous address: XXXXX, Palm Harbor and XXXX, Oldsmar

VEHICLE: 1990 Ford F150, two-tone tan/brown, tinted windows, large chrome roll bar, FL tag also has a **suspended driver license.**

Since December 25th, 1998 there have been **nine** incidents of exposure of sex organs occurring mostly at apartment complexes and condominiums within and surrounding the **Eastlake Woodlands area.** The latest incident occurred at Old Republic Title Company. When the victim looked, the suspect was crouched down outside the window with his shirt over his head. He stood up with his pants past his waistline and fled when the victim screamed. All of the previous incidents have occurred at residences between the hours of 19:00 and 22:00. The suspect stands outside, sometimes knocking on the patio door, until he has the victim's attention. He covers his face with a cloth or shirt and when the victim looks, he usually masturbates and flees when they scream.

Suspect Description: W/M, early twenties, thin to medium build, 5-10, 165, and brown hair. One victim described him as having "bulgy" eyes, is sometimes completely naked, and on other occasions has been seen wearing a dark shirt and shorts, sunglasses, a sweatshirt, blue/white striped shirt, Docker pants, and once wearing gym shorts. He may be riding a bicycle or lives nearby, as a track hasn't been established by K9.

The following is a listing of reports and addresses in order of occurrence:

	RPT #	DATE	DAY	F/TIME	GRID	STREET LOCATION
#1	98-273692	12/25/1998	FRI	20.25	157	xxx CYPRESS LN
#2	98-273735	12/25/1998	FRI	21.75	145	xxx LIFESTYLE BLVD APT 310
#3	99-4090	01/06/1999	WED	19.50	168	xxx COUNTRYSIDE KEY BLVD
#4	99-15113	01/22/1999	FRI	21.75	168	xxx COUNTRYSIDE KEY BLVD
#5	99-22451	01/31/1999	SUN	20.00	157	xx WOODLAKE PL
#6	99-28838	02/09/1999	TUE	20.45	157	xxx CYPRESS CT
#7	99-45403	03/04/1999	THUR	22.00	157	xxx CYPRESS CT
#8	99-66785	04/02/1999	FRI	21.25	157	xxx CYPRESS LN
#9	99-70724	04/07/1999	WED	22.00	157	xxx TAMPA RD

UPDATED FORECAST: If all circumstances remain the same, there is a 68 percent probability the suspect will strike again **between April 13th and May 1st** and most likely **between 19:00 and 22:00 hours,** within the targeted area. See page two for map.

EXTRA PATROL and **INCREASED FIRs** are requested for the described area, particularly within apartment complexes and condominiums. Refer all information to Sergeant M. Ring, Crimes Against Persons, 582-6307 and Detective M. Bailey, NDS Burglary Unit, 582-6947.

TARGETED AREA

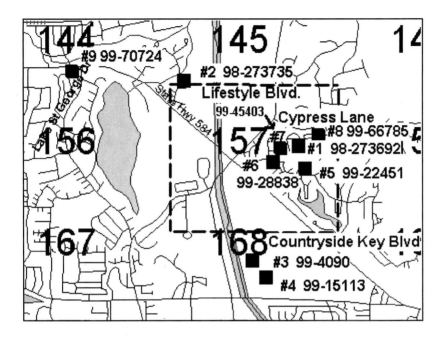

Bibliography

Anderson, R. (1997). Intelligence-Led Policing: A British Perspective. In A. Smith (Ed.), *Intelligence-Led Policing: International Perspectives on Policing in the 21st Century* (pp. 5-8). Lawrenceville, NJ: International Association of Law Enforcement Intelligence Analysts.

Atkin, H.N. (1998). Keeping It Simple: A Practitioner's Approach to Applying the Intelligence Process, from Formulating Premises to Recommendation. *IALEIA Journal, 2*(2): 1-11.

Atkin, H.N. (1999). A New National Intelligence Model for the UK. In A. Hopkins (Ed.), *Intelligence Models and Best Practices* (pp. 29-33). Lawrenceville, NJ: International Association of Law Enforcement Intelligence Analysts.

Atkin, H.N. (2000). Criminal Intelligence Analysis: A Scientific Perspective. *IALEIA Journal, 13*(1): 1-15.

Bailey, D.H. and Shearing, C.D. (1998). The Future of Policing. In G.F. Cole and M.G. Gertz (Eds.), *The Criminal Justice System: Politics and Policies* (pp. 150-167). Belmont, CA: Wadsworth Publishing Company.

Basara, J. (1997). Intelligence-Led Policing in the United States: A Software Vendor's View. In A. Smith (Ed.), *Intelligence-Led Policing: International Perspectives on Policing in the 21st Century* (pp. 24-26). Lawrenceville, NJ: International Association of Law Enforcement Intelligence Analysts.

Bennet, W.W. and Hess, K.M. (1998). *Criminal Investigation.* Belmont, CA: Wadsworth Publishing Company.

Blaney, A. (1999). Information Gap. *IALEIA Journal,* February: 53-57.

Block, C.R., Dabdoub, M., and Fregly, S. (1995). *Crime Analysis Through Computer Mapping.* Washington, DC: Police Executive Research Forum.

Block, C.R. and Green, L.A. (1994). *The Geoarchive Handbook: A Guide for Developing a Geographic Database As an Information Foundation for Community Policing.* Chicago, IL: Illinois Criminal Justice Information Authority.

Boba, R. (1999). Using the Internet to Disseminate Crime Information. *FBI Law Enforcement Bulletin 68*(10): 6-9.

Bratton, W. (1998). *Turnaround.* New York: Random House.

Burton, G.J. (2000). Presentation on FBI Analysts' Competencies. June 7, 2000, at Mercyhurst College, Erie, PA.

California State Department of Labor (1999). *Crime and Intelligence Analysts.* California Occupational Guide Number 557. Available online: <http://www.calmis.cahwnet.gov/file/occguide/CRIMANLT.HTM>.

Canter, P. (1995). State of the Statistical Art: Point Pattern Analysis. In C.R. Block, M. Dabdoub, and S. Fregy (Eds.), *Crime Analysis Through Computer Mapping* (pp. 151-160). Washington, DC: Police Executive Research Forum.

Casady, T. (1999). Privacy Issues in the Presentation of Geocoded Data. *Crime Mapping News 1*(3): 1-3, 8.

Chalmers, A.F. (1982). *What Is This Thing Called Science?* Indianapolis, IN: Hackett Publishing Co.

Cole, G.F. and Gertz, M.G. (1998). *The Criminal Justice System: Politics and Policies.* Belmont, CA: Wadsworth Publishing Company.

Collins, P.I., Johnson, G.F., Choy, A., Davidson, K.T., and Mackay, R.E. (1998). Advances in Violent Crime Analysis and Law Enforcement: The Canadian Violent Crime Linkage Analysis System. *Journal of Government Information 25*(3), 277-284.

Commission on Accreditation for Law Enforcement Agencies, Inc. (1994). *Standards for Law Enforcement Agencies: The Standards Manual of the Law Enforcement Agency Accreditation Program.* Fairfax, VA: CALEA.

Coplink: Database Detective (1999). *National Law Enforcement and Corrections Center, Tech Beat,* pp. 1-2.

Crime Statistics Don't Tell the Whole Story (1999). *Community Policing Exchange IV*(29): 1-2.

Davenport, T.H. and Prusek, L. (2000). *Working Knowledge: How Organizations Manage What They Know.* Boston: Harvard Business School Press.

Davis, J. (1998). *Criminal Behavioral Assessment Protocol: The Stalker.* Paper presented at the annual International Association of Crime Analysts conference in San Diego, CA, November.

Dewey, J. (1997). *How We Think.* Toronto: Dover Publications, Inc.

Downing, D. and Clark, J. (1997). *Statistics: The Easy Way.* New York: Barron's Educational Series, Inc.

Duvenage, D. (2000). Presentation on Research and Intelligence Training in the Intelligence Academy of South Africa on June 7, 2000, at Mercyhurst College, Erie, PA.

Evans, R.M. (2000). Presentation on intelligence analysis issues in the Royal Ulster Constabulary Analysis Centre on June 7, 2000, at Mercyhurst College, Erie, PA.

Fagan, J., Dumanovsky, J., Thompson, J.P., and Davies, G. (1998). Crime in Public Housing: Clarifying Research Issues. *National Institute of Justice Journal,* March.

Fahlman, R. (1998). Human Resources and Crime Analysis: Selection, Recruitment, and Training. *IALEIA Journal 11*(1): 36-42.

Forst, B. (1995). The Analytics of Criminal Investigation: Putting Sherlock Holmes in a Box. *IALEIA Journal 9*(2).

Gebhardt, C.S. (1999). Crime Analysis: The Next Phase. *Police Chief,* April: 33-39.

Geller, W.A. (1997). Suppose We Were Really Serious About Police Departments Becoming "Learning Organizations"? *National Institute of Justice Journal,* December. <http://ncjrs.org/txtfiles/jr000234.txt>.

Geney, M. (1997). Regional Crime Analysis Project. *Central Virginia Criminal Justice News,* Summer: 1-3.

Gladwell, M. (2000). *The Tipping Point: How Little Things Can Make a Big Difference.* Boston: Little, Brown and Company.

Goldstein, H. (1990). *Problem-Oriented Policing.* Philadelphia: Temple University.

Gottlieb, S.L., Arenberg, S., and Singh, R. (1994). *Crime Analysis: From First Report to Final Arrest.* Montclair, CA: Alpha Publishing.

Haley, K.N., Todd, J.C., and Stallo, M. (1998). *Crime Analysis and the Struggle for Legitimacy.* Available online: <http://www.iaca.net/resources/articles/legitimacy.html>.

Hall, R. (1999). Intelligence-Led Policing and the Role of the Analyst. *IALEIA Journal,* August: 39-46.

Harries, K. (1999). *Mapping Crime: Principle and Practice.* Washington, DC: U.S. Department of Justice.

Hartnett, S.M. and Skogan, W.G. (1999). Community Policing: Chicago's Experience. *National Institute of Justice Journal* 239(April): 3-11.

Heibel, R. (1997). Who's Going to Mine the Information Klondike? *Colloquy,* April: 10-11, 29-30.

Helms, D. (1999). The Use of Dynamic Spatio-Temporal Analytical Techniques to Resolve Emergent Crime Series. Paper presented at the Third Annual Crime Mapping Research Center conference in Orlando, Florida, December.

Helms, D. (2000). Trendspotting: Serial Crime Detection with GIS. *Crime Mapping News* 2(2): 5-8.

Heuer, R.J. (1999). *Psychology of Intelligence Analysis.* Center for the Study of Intelligence, Central Intelligence Agency. Available online: <http://www.cia.gov/csi/books/19104/>.

Holman, D. (2000). Presentation on National Criminal Intelligence Service's training standard for analysts in the United Kingdom on June 7, 2000, at Mercyhurst College, Erie, PA.

Hopkins, A. (Ed.) (1999). *Intelligence Models and Best Practices.*Lawrenceville, NJ: International Association of Law Enforcement Intelligence Analysts.

Hughes, K. (2000). Implementing a GIS Application: Lessons Learned in a Law Enforcement Environment. *Crime Mapping News* 2(1): 1-5.

Hutton, S.A. and Myrent, M. (1999). *Incident-Based Crime Analysis Manual: Utilizing Local-Level Incident Reports for Solving Crimes.* Chicago: Illinois Criminal Justice Information Authority.

IACP's National Law Enforcement Policy Center (1994). *The Model Policy on Crime Analysis.* Washington, DC: International Association of Chiefs of Police.

IACP's National Law Enforcement Policy Center (1998). *The Model Policy on Intelligence.* Washington, DC: International Association of Chiefs of Police.

International Association of Law Enforcement Intelligence Analysts (1996). *Successful Law Enforcement Using Analytical Methods.* Richmond, VA: IALEIA, Inc.

International Association of Law Enforcement Intelligence Analysts (1997). *Guidelines for Starting an Analytical Unit.* Richmond, VA: IALEIA, Inc.

James, D. (1988). *Practical Statistics for Police Supervisors.* Handout presented to Dallas Police Department Supervisory Class. Southwestern Law Enforcement Institute.

Johnson, A.P. (1999). Community Policing and Intelligence Measuring Client Satisfaction. In A. Hopkins (Ed.), *Intelligence Models and Best Practices* (pp. 5-8).

Lawrenceville, NJ: International Association of Law Enforcement Intelligence Analysts.

Kahaner, L. (1996). *Competitive Intelligence: How to Gather, Analyze, and Use Information to Move Your Business to the Top.* New York: Touchtone-Simon & Schuster, Inc.

Kerlinger, F.N. (1977). *Foundations of Behavioral Research.* New York: Holt, Rinehart and Winston, Inc.

Kimminau, J. (1999). Certification Update. *IACA Forecaster,* Winter: 3, 6.

Klofas, J. and Stojkovic, S. (1995). *Crime and Justice in the Year 2010.* Belmont, CA: Wadswoth Publishing Company.

Knight, M. (1997). Tactical Crime Analysis. In M.M. Reuland (Ed.), *Information Management and Crime Analysis: Practitioner's Recipes for Success* (pp. 25-37). Washington, DC: Police Executive Research Forum.

Krattenmaker, J.L. (1999). A Model of Open Source Information. In A. Hopkins (Ed.), *Intelligence Models and Best Practices* (pp. 31-38). Lawrenceville, NJ: International Association of Law Enforcement Intelligence Analysts.

Krizan, L. (1999). *Intelligence Essentials for Everyone.* Occasional Paper Number Six. Washington, DC: Joint Military Intelligence College.

La Vigne, N.G. (1999). Computerized Mapping As a Tool for Problem-Oriented Policing. *Crime Mapping News 1*(1): 1-3.

La Vigne, N.G. and Wartell, J. (Eds.) (1998). *Crime Mapping Case Studies: Successes in the Field* (Volume 1). Washington, DC: Police Executive Research Forum.

La Vigne, N.G. and Wartell, J. (Eds.) (2000). *Crime Mapping Case Studies: Successes in the Field* (Volume 2). Washington, DC: Police Executive Research Forum.

Lambert, B. (1996). Data Warehousing Fundamentals: What You Need to Know to Succeed. *DMReview.com.* Available online: <http://dmreview.com/master.cfm?NavID=198&EdID=1313>.

Law Enforcement Management and Administrative Statistics (1999). *Bureau of Justice Statistics Executive Summary.* Washington, DC: U.S. Department of Justice.

LeBeuf, M. (2000). *Policing and Use of Information Technology: An Assessment.* Ottawa: Canadian Police College.

Leedy, P.D. (1997). *Practical Research: Planning and Design.* Upper Saddle River, NJ: Prentice-Hall, Inc.

Lewin, J. (1997). Decentralized Crime Analysis by the Beat Officer. In M.M. Reuland (Ed.), *Information Management and Crime Analysis: Practitioner's Recipes for Success* (pp. 39-50). Washington, DC: Police Executive Research Forum.

Lipsky, M. (1998). Toward a Theory of Street-Level Bureaucracy. In G.F. Cole and M.G. Gertz (Eds.), *The Criminal Justice System: Politics and Policies* (pp. 24-40). Belmont, CA: Wadsworth Publishing Company.

Los Angeles County Sheriff's Department (1999). *1998 Crime Analysis Program Annual Report.*

Maber, A. (2000). The "Location Advantage"—The Application of GIS Technology by the New South Wales Police Service. *Jane's International Police Review,* January/February.

MacKay, R. (1999). Geographic Profiling: A New Tool for Law Enforcement. *The Police Chief,* December: 51-59.

Maguire, K. and Pastore, A.L. (Eds.) (1999). *Sourcebook of Criminal Justice Statistics 1998.* Washington, DC: U.S. Department of Justice, Bureau of Justice Statistics-USGPO.

Making Information Technology Work (2000). *Tech Beat.* Rockville, MD: National Law Enforcement and Corrections Technology Center.

McCormick, D. (1999). Crime Analysts Enhance Community Policing Efforts. *Tampa Tribune,* pp. 90-91.

McEwen, T. (1999). NIJ's Locally Initiated Research Partnerships in Policing: Factors That Add up to Success. *National Institute of Justice Journal 238*(January): 2-10.

Meese, E. III (1993). Community Policing and the Police Officer. *Perspectives on Policing.* January.

Miller, T. (1995). Integrating Crime Mapping with CAD and RMS. In C.R. Block, M. Dabdoub, and S. Fregy (Eds.), *Crime Analysis Through Computer Mapping* (pp. 179-188). Washington, DC: Police Executive Research Forum.

Monmonier, M. (1996). *How to Lie with Maps.* Chicago: The University of Chicago Press.

Morgan, D.J. (1998). *The Thinker's Toolkit: 14 Powerful Techniques for Problem Solving.* New York: Times Business-Random House.

Moriarty, L. and Carter, D. (1998). *Criminal Justice Technology in the 21st Century.* Illinois: Charles C Thomas.

Morris, J. (1993). *Crime Analysis Charting: Visual Investigative Analysis, Link Analysis, Telephone Toll Analysis.* Loomis, CA: The Palmer Press.

Morrison, R.D. (1997). Cyber-Investigator—The New Detective. *Law Enforcement Technology,* August: 56-58.

Morton, A. (1997). *A Guide Through the Theory of Knowledge.* Malden, MA: Blackwell Publishers, Inc.

Nakamura, R. and Smallwood, F. (1980). *The Politics of Policy Implementation.* New York: St. Martin's Press.

Nath, P. (1999). *Crime Mapping—A Multifaceted Tool—The German Approach.* Paper presented at the Third Annual International Crime Mapping Research Center conference, Orlando Florida.

National Criminal Intelligence Service (2000). *The National Intelligence Model.* London: NCIS.

Peterson, M. (1997). The Role of Analysis in Intelligence-Led Policing. In A. Smith (Ed.), *Intelligence-Led Policing: International Perspectives on Policing in the 21st Century* (pp. 2-4). Lawrenceville, NJ: International Association of Law Enforcement Intelligence Analysts.

Peterson, M. (1998). *Applications in Criminal Analysis: A Sourcebook.* Westport, CT: Greenwood Press.

Peterson, M. (1998). Joining the Debate: Product vs. Process. *IALEIA Journal 11*(1): 1-13.

Pilant, L. (1997). Computerized Crime Mapping. *The Police Chief,* December: 60-69.

Pilant, L. (1999). Crime Mapping and Analysis. *The Police Chief,* December: 38-49.

Pollock, J.M. (1998). *Ethics in Crime and Justice.* Belmont, CA: Wadsworth Publishing Company.

Porter, R.M. (1997). Getting Started in Intelligence-Led Policing. In A. Smith (Ed.), *Intelligence-Led Policing: International Perspectives on Policing in the 21st Century* (pp. 27-33). Lawrenceville, NJ: International Association of Law Enforcement Intelligence Analysts.

Porter, R.M. (1999). Iowa's LEIN Program Offers Law Enforcement "Excellence Through Corporation." In A. Hopkins (Ed.), *Intelligence Models and Best Practices* (pp. 23-28). Lawrenceville, NJ: International Association of Law Enforcement Intelligence Analysts.

Potter, V.G. (1994). *On Understanding Understanding: A Philosophy of Knowledge.* New York: Fordham University Press.

Radcliffe, J.R. (2002). Intelligence-Led Policing and the Problems of Turning Rhetoric into Practice. *Policing and Society 12*(1): 53-66.

Reiter, M.S. (1999). Empowerment Policing. *FBI LAW Enforcement Bulletin, 68*(2): 7-11.

Research/Intelligence Analyst Program (2000). *Intelligence-Related Law Enforcement Training Guide.* Sponsored by Lexis-Nexis Group. Erie, PA: Mercyhurst College.

Reuland, M.M. (Ed.) (1997). *Information Management and Crime Analysis: Practitioner's Recipes for Success.* Washington, DC: Police Executive Research Forum.

Rich, T.F. (1995). The Use of Computerized Mapping in Crime Control and Prevention Programs. NIJ Research in Action Series. Available online: <http://ncjrs.org/txtfiles/riamap.txt>.

Rich, T.F. (1999). Mapping the Path to Problem Solving. *National Institute of Justice Journal 241*(October): 1-9.

Robertson, S. (1997). Intelligence-Led Policing: a European Union View. In A. Smith (Ed.), *Intelligence-Led Policing: International Perspectives on Policing in the 21st Century* (pp. 21-23). Lawrenceville, NJ: International Association of Law Enforcement Intelligence Analysts.

Rogers, D. (2000). Getting a slice of the pie. *Law Enforcement Technology,* March: 18-22.

Rogers, D. (2000). Trends in crime analysis and crime mapping. *Law Enforcement Technology,* May: 36-42.

Rossmo, D.K. (2000). *Geographic Profiling.* Boca Raton, FL: CRC Press.

Ryan, M.A. (1999). The Future Role of a State Intelligence Program. *IALEIA Journal, 12*(2): 28-47.

Sadd, S. and Grinc, R.M. (1996). Implementation Challenges in Community Policing: Innovative Neighborhood-Oriented Policing in Eight Cities. *National Institute of Justice: Research in Brief,* February: Washington, DC: U.S. Department of Justice.

Sanford, R. (1995). How to Develop a Tactical Early Warning System on a Small-City Budget. In C.R. Block, M. Dabdoub, and S. Fregy (Eds.), *Crime Analysis*

Through Computer Mapping (pp. 199-208). Washington, DC: Police Executive Research Forum.

Schoenle, G.W. (1999). *Technology and Policing in "2000."* Unpublished manuscript.

Schuster, L. (2000). The National Concept of Crime Intelligence Analysis in Germany: Current Status and Progress. *IALEIA Journal 13*(1): 16-31.

Seaskate, Inc. (1997). *The Evolution and Development of Police Technology.* Prepared for the National Institute of Justice Office of Science and Technology.

Skolnick, J.H. (1998). A Sketch of the Policeman's "Working Personality." In G.F. Cole and M.G. Gertz (Eds.), *The Criminal Justice System: Politics and Policies* (pp. 116-133). Belmont, CA: Wadsworth Publishing Company.

Smith, A. (Ed.) (1997). *Intelligence-Led Policing: International Perspectives on Policing in the 21st Century.* Lawrenceville, NJ: International Association of Law Enforcement Intelligence Analysts.

Smith, A. (1997). Towards Intelligence-Led Policing: The RCMP Experience. In A. Smith (Ed.), *Intelligence-Led Policing: International Perspectives on Policing in the 21st Century.* Lawrenceville, NJ: International Association of Law Enforcement Intelligence Analysts.

Soulliere, N. (1999). *Police and Technology: Historical Review and Current Status.* Ottawa: Canadian Police College.

Spelman, W.G. (1987). *Beyond Bean Counting: New Approaches for Managing Crime Data.* Washington, DC: Police Executive Research Forum.

Stallo, M. (1997). Crime Analysis: The Administrative Function. In M.M. Reuland (Ed.), *Information Management and Crime Analysis: Practitioner's Recipes for Success* (pp. 63-76). Washington, DC: Police Executive Research Forum.

Stewart, T.A. (1998). *Intellectual Capital: The New Wealth of Organizations.* New York: Bantam Books.

Surette, R. (1998). *Media, Crime, and Criminal Justice: Images and Realities.* Belmont, CA: Wadsworth Publishing Company.

Sutton, J.R. (2000). *Subversion of Government Monopoly: The Privatization of Intelligence Services.* Resources for Intelligence Management Evolution Series. Erie, PA: Research Intelligence Consortium, Inc.

Swanson, C.R., Chamelin, N.C., and Territo, L. (2000). *Criminal Investigation.* Boston, MA: McGraw-Hill.

Sweeney, W. (1998). Analyst Training Survey Reveals Need for Revamp; Growing Interest in Certification. *IALEIA Intelscope,* September: 1, 3.

Taylor, D.L. (1999). The Role of Analysts—As We Approach the 21st Century. . . An IALEIA Survey. *IALEIA Journal 12*(2): 1-17.

Thomas, R. (1999). Free Maps to Drug Enforcement Agencies from the National Guard. *Crime Mapping News 1*(2): 1-2.

Tully, E.J. and McKee, S. (2000). *The Present and Future Use of the Internet by Law Enforcement: Part One.* A report for the Major Cities Chiefs, FBI Academy, and the National Executive Institute Associates.

Turvey, B.E. (1999). *Criminal Profiling: An Introduction to Behavioral Evidence Analysis.* San Diego: Academic Press.

United States Department of Justice (1999). Mapping Out Crime: Providing 21st Century Tools for Safe Communities. *Report of the Task Force on Crime Mapping and Data Driven Management.* Available online: <http://govinfo.library.unt.edu/npr/library/papers/bkgrd/crimemap/content.html>.

Velasco, M. and Boba, R. (2000). Tactical Crime Analysis and Geographic Information Systems: Concepts and Examples. *Crime Mapping News* 2(2): 1-4.

Waller, I. and Welsh, B.C. (1998). Reducing Crime by Harnessing International Best Practice. *National Institute of Justice Journal* 237(October): 26-31.

Weiss, A. (1999). Informal Information Sharing Among Police Agencies. *National Institute of Justice Journal* 238(January): 25-26.

White House Task Force (2000). *General Counterdrug Intelligence Plan.* Washington, DC: USGPO. Available online: <http://www.whitehousedrugpolicy.gov/publications/gcip/index.html>.

Wilson, J.Q. and Kelling, G.L. (1998). Broken Windows: The Police and Neighborhood Safety. In G.F. Cole and M.G. Gertz (Eds.), *The Criminal Justice System: Politics and Policies* (pp. 101-115). Belmont, CA: Wadsworth Publishing Company.

Witkin, G. (1998). The Crime Bust. *U.S. News and World Report,* May 25, pp. 28-40.

Index

Page numbers followed by the letter "t" indicate tables.

SPECIAL 25%-OFF DISCOUNT!
Order a copy of this book with this form or online at:
http://www.haworthpressinc.com/store/product.asp?sku=4852

INTRODUCTION TO CRIME ANALYSIS
Basic Resources for Criminal Justice Practice

_____in hardbound at $37.46 (regularly $49.95) (ISBN: 0-7890-1867-5)

_____in softbound at $13.46 (regularly $17.95) (ISBN: 0-7890-1868-3)

Or order online and use Code HEC25 in the shopping cart.

COST OF BOOKS_____

OUTSIDE US/CANADA/
MEXICO: ADD 20%_____

POSTAGE & HANDLING_____
(US: $5.00 for first book & $2.00
for each additional book)
Outside US: $6.00 for first book
& $2.00 for each additional book)

SUBTOTAL_____

IN CANADA: ADD 7% GST_____

STATE TAX_____
(NY, OH & MN residents, please
add appropriate local sales tax)

FINAL TOTAL_____
(If paying in Canadian funds,
convert using the current
exchange rate, UNESCO
coupons welcome)

☐ **BILL ME LATER:** ($5 service charge will be added)
(Bill-me option is good on US/Canada/Mexico orders only;
not good to jobbers, wholesalers, or subscription agencies.)

☐ Check here if billing address is different from
shipping address and attach purchase order and
billing address information.

Signature_____

☐ **PAYMENT ENCLOSED: $**_____

☐ **PLEASE CHARGE TO MY CREDIT CARD.**

☐ Visa ☐ MasterCard ☐ AmEx ☐ Discover
☐ Diner's Club ☐ Eurocard ☐ JCB

Account # _____

Exp. Date_____

Signature_____

Prices in US dollars and subject to change without notice.

NAME_____

INSTITUTION_____

ADDRESS_____

CITY_____

STATE/ZIP_____

COUNTRY_____ COUNTY (NY residents only)_____

TEL_____ FAX_____

E-MAIL_____

May we use your e-mail address for confirmations and other types of information? ☐ Yes ☐ No
We appreciate receiving your e-mail address and fax number. Haworth would like to e-mail or fax special
discount offers to you, as a preferred customer. **We will never share, rent, or exchange your e-mail address
or fax number.** We regard such actions as an invasion of your privacy.

Order From Your Local Bookstore or Directly From
The Haworth Press, Inc.
10 Alice Street, Binghamton, New York 13904-1580 • USA
TELEPHONE: 1-800-HAWORTH (1-800-429-6784) / Outside US/Canada: (607) 722-5857
FAX: 1-800-895-0582 / Outside US/Canada: (607) 722-6362
E-mail to: getinfo@haworthpressinc.com
PLEASE PHOTOCOPY THIS FORM FOR YOUR PERSONAL USE.